Beyond the
Wax Strip

The secret life of a beauty therapist

By Wendy Freeman

For my clients
I couldn't have done it without you

Table of Contents

Introduction to my world

I've been a beauty therapist for thirty years. It's been an amazing career that has brought me great joy throughout my working life.

It's been a role that no matter how low I've felt it has always lifted me up, even in life's difficult times. I'm not the only therapist to feel this way either. Time and again in surveys, beauty therapy comes out in the top three (and often in first place) on the scale of happiness at work.

Why are we so happy in our work? Well, I hope my little book will help answer that question.

Beauticians, as we're often called, tend to be stereotyped. We're often considered a bit blonde. In other words, we're not seen as highly intelligent. People think of us as having hair extensions down to our bums, artificial talons for nails, make-up caked on and bright orange, fake tans. I think they see us as Barbie Dolls.

Our jobs can be perceived as rather shallow too. People seem to think we spend our days chatting aimlessly, applying make-up, and gossiping with each other about our clients.

As with any profession there are these that let the side down. Unfortunately, there are beauty therapists who are vein, covered in inch thick make-up and they do gossip about their clients. But for me and the therapists I've worked with this description is not at all accurate.

As for the long talons and blonde hair, that isn't me at all. I'm only five foot two and not one blonde hair in sight. I never have long nails because they get in the way of me giving a good massage. I hardly wear any make-up and have even been told off for not wearing enough on some occasions. I was just not glamorous enough for some places.

Although I'm not Mensa material, neither am I stupid. Unlike a certain *The Only Way is Essex* therapist; my geography is rather good, and I do realise that Pakistan is not the capital of India.

I am exceptional at my job and have always made a point of keeping up with the latest treatments and breakthroughs in the industry. I've made a real difference in many people's lives. With my knowledge of the skin I've improved some really debilitating skin diseases and disorders.

Often people have an interest in my work and there is a real curiosity about the beauty profession. I am always quick to tell them the job is not at all glamorous and I like to re-educate them on the negative beautician image. I've always told people that it's a lot harder work than they could imagine; with long days, no tea-breaks and often having to grab lunch on the go.

I start the day looking good, with my hair dressed and make-up in place, but by the end of the day, I usually look like I've been pulled through a hedge backwards.

Some people also think I spend my life lying on a treatment couch, being pampered. This is, in fact, as far from the truth as you could possibly get. I'm normally the last in line for treatments. Often, I'm found walking around with one leg waxed and the other left hairy for weeks at a time. This is either because I don't have the time to finish the wax or because a young therapist has been practising on me.

But I've never cared about that because for me, it's always been the job that was most important, along with the clients and my fellow therapists.

If you met me, I would enthusiastically tell you about all the great variety of people I've met from all walks of life. Many of whom I admire greatly, and you'll meet some of them in the following pages. I've met and treated people from all parts of society, from the working classes to the rich and famous. I've adored working with them all.

Working closely, and often intimately, with so many people daily I often realise that no matter how bad you think your life is there is always someone who has a heavier load to carry.

No matter what has been going on in my personal life, as soon as I step into the salon, the smile goes on and I am instantly happy and professional. It's a little like being on stage; nobody wants to go to a miserable therapist.

The plus side of this is usually when you pretend to be happy, you become happy. This is a great practise that has served me well and kept me sane for many years.

I'm incredibly grateful to have chosen beauty therapy as my career. Over the years I've always chatted to my clients; often telling them funny stories about the profession to put them at ease.

So many of them have said, "You should write a book", and I always said, "I will one day."

Well this is my one day and here I am, giving you the low down on this amazingly diverse and fascinating profession. I'll tell you a little about the treatments, lots about the clients, some very funny stories and a few rather gross ones too.

Most of the anecdotes have happened to me personally. However, a few have happened to other therapists who have gleefully shared them with me. To keep things simple, I've written their stories as though they were my own. They could have just as easily been so. But I do promise you, everything you are about to read really happened.

The names of the clients are not real as confidentiality is important in this profession. I hope my clients will understand that I'm not making fun of them. Please also bear in mind that some of these tales could have happened on more than one occasion, so although you may think it's your story, it might not be you at all.

I hope you enjoy this unique insight into my wonderful profession.

The Beginning

The idea for my wonderful career began way back in August 1982. I had just left secondary school and was looking forward to a summer of freedom. No school, no job, just a lush boyfriend and lots of partying.

Everyone was asking me the same question, "What do you want to do?" But at fifteen I just didn't have a clue. The only option I could see for myself at that time was to go to college.

After all, I would only have to work until I got married and had kids. An ideal job would mean I worked until I had my first child. Then, hopefully, the job would flow into something I could do from home. It sounds unreal nowadays, but that's how it was back then. Most girls were brought up to get married and have kids. That was our career.

At school we were all told to book an appointment with a Careers Adviser, and they would tell us what to do next. This was quite modern compared to when my mum left school. She was simply sent off to Woolworths to work.

Off I went to find out what my ideal job would be. I answered a few questions on a computer and within minutes I was told what my future career looked like.

Whilst taking the test I was more interested in my boyfriend, Paul, and our forthcoming night out together. I was hardly concentrating on the questions at all. I was filling in the answers with one hand and checking my watch with the other.

My Careers Adviser analysed the results, sat me down smiling sweetly, and said, "What a lovely caring young lady you are". I looked around to check if she was talking to me; and then looked back and noticed her fingernails. They really were a mess.

"You need to go into a caring profession: social worker or nurse would be ideal." These results were not what I expected, and I suddenly thought that maybe I should have answered the questions a little more honestly. I was certainly not nurse-quality back then. I couldn't stand the sight of blood and I certainly didn't want to be surrounded by sick people.

Anyway, social work and nursing were out of the question once the advisor realised my grades were less than perfect. There were no A-levels on the horizon and no chance of university for me. So, she concluded that I would be an ideal candidate to work with children or the elderly.

I didn't bother telling her that I didn't particularly like kids. And I had already done some voluntary work in an elderly home and hated it. Besides, time was ticking on and I needed to get home, paint my nails, and get ready for my Friday night out.

So, to keep her happy, I agreed I would go to the college and sign-up for either a Child Care or Community Care course. She was happy her job was done, and I was happy to be leaving. A fifteen-year old's priorities are often a bit wonky to say the least.

Monday morning came and as promised, I did go to the college, but signed up for Bookkeeping & Basic Office Skills instead. The logic behind my decision was that I enjoyed typing class in school and I could work from home once I had children.

Luckily bookkeeping would not be my fate thanks to one lady I had the good fortune to know. She would, inadvertently, change my career path by introducing me to the beauty industry.

CB radio (Citizens Band) was immensely popular in the eighties. It was like social media networking before Twitter and Facebook. You talked to friends and strangers using a radio set. The big aerials on the roof of your house and car gave you access to chit-chat with anyone else who had a CB radio.

We all had call signs instead of using our own names. This was a necessity. Unlike Facebook you couldn't adjust your privacy settings. Nothing was private. There was nowhere to post profile pictures, so to put faces to the names we would meet up for an 'Eyeball'. Yes, everything was in code, even meeting up for a drink.

This was where I met a fellow CBer, 'Lady C'. She was older than me and I thought she was extremely glamorous. She always wore stunning outfits and her make-up was perfect. It was subtle, not the usual black eyes and blue eye shadow seen at this time. Her skin was a beautiful golden colour, as she even had her very own sun bed.

Lady C asked me what I would be doing now I had finished school. I told her, bookkeeping, as my typing was good, and I could work from home when I got married and had kids.

She replied, "I can't see you in an office, and why do something just because it's convenient for starting a family. Do something you love. What about working in a beauty salon? Your fingernails always look great."

I told her I wasn't interested in hairdressing. Then she explained, she wasn't talking about hairdressing but a beautician in a salon. "I go to a lovely little salon in Chippenham for my nails, hair removal and some other tweaks", she told me.

I was impressed. Up until then I didn't know anyone who went to a beauty salon for treatments. She was married and had kids. I just assumed from the way I was brought up that housewives didn't go to beauty salons. Only film stars did that.

A couple of weeks later I had a phone call from Lady C telling me the salon she'd mentioned was looking for an apprentice. I excitedly called about the position straight away and they offered me an interview.

I can still remember the smart, red dress I wore and how grown-up I felt. The interview was marvellous. The manageress showed me around, explaining, one day a week would be spent studying at college, and the rest of the time would be in the salon working on clients. She talked about waxing, skincare, and eyelash tints; stuff I had never heard of. She praised my skin as well as my nails. "You're just what we're looking for." she said.

I knew she was impressed, and we spoke about a second interview. It was so thrilling, and I thought it was an amazing opportunity. But suddenly she realised she hadn't asked me my age, and that was when the blow came.

There would be no second interview and no apprenticeship. She had thought I was at least nineteen. What a huge disappointment. I was told to come back in a few years, which at fifteen seemed a lifetime away.

Looking back at the situation now, the idea of a fifteen-year-old working on a client is unthinkable. Most of the clientele would have consisted of ladies over the age of forty. I doubt if they would have appreciated a young teenager waxing their bikini line.

Despite my disappointment, the seed had been sown. I had fallen in love with the idea of becoming a beautician.

In the meantime, I went to college and started my bookkeeping course. I only lasted two months. I hated sitting behind a desk all day, trying to balance numbers in a book. Even the typing was tedious, listening to invisible people, dictating stuff I didn't understand into my headphones.

I soon quit and got a job in a supermarket instead. I was sixteen and engaged by then, so who needed a career?

The engagement didn't last long. Unfortunately, the job seemed to last forever. I was just plodding along in a daze, sitting all day long, pushing the keys of an old-fashioned till. There were some aspects of the job I enjoyed, such as meeting different people and getting to know the regulars. But it was so boring. I could do the work with my eyes closed or even slightly drunk. And on more than one occasion my boss and I indulged in boozy lunches just to get through the boredom of the afternoon.

Although I knew one day, I would get married and have children, I also knew I wanted a job I loved. And the supermarket definitely wasn't it. This was the eighties, and more and more women were working and building their own careers at the same times as having families. I couldn't get out of my head how excited I had felt in that beauty salon. I decided I wouldn't settle for a job that was going nowhere. I wanted to be a beauty therapist. I wanted a career!

Unlike the previous decades, people now had disposable income to spend on themselves. This was the age of the YUPPY! Beauty regimes were becoming popular and suddenly more people were going to salons for treatments. This meant more demand for therapists. But the salons wanted them ready trained, with proper qualifications. They no longer found it acceptable to have an apprentice working on their clients.

Looking back, it must have been a disaster allowing unqualified therapists to practise on the poor paying customers. When I had my own salon years later, I was always reluctant to let newly qualified therapists loose on clients. I needed to be a hundred percent sure they were able to carry out the job properly. One mistake and you've lost a client forever.

How was I going to become a beauty therapist though? Perhaps go back to college? I needed some advice to realise my dream. So, once again, I headed to the Careers Advisor.

This time I marched in knowing full well what I wanted. Unfortunately, she just tried to push me into taking a full-time hair and beauty course, even though I wasn't interested in becoming a hairdresser. In her opinion I would struggle to get work having studied only beauty. Most of the salons were hairdressers with a beauty section on the side, so she thought this would be the sensible option.

Have you ever been so sure of something that you'd bet your life savings on it, and just know you were about to win?

I was older now and much more assertive on this visit and told the Career Advisor with absolute certainty. "You mark my words, in ten years' time there will be a beauty salon on every street and I'm going to own one!"

Eventually I prised the advice from her of how to achieve my goal. I would have to study part time in the evenings and finance the courses myself.

So, my learning journey and my career began. This was one of the best decisions I've ever made and all thanks to CB radio, and Lady C.

Lost Opportunities

I've always loved my work. Over the course of my career I've worked in high-street salons, as a mobile therapist, in a spa, at home in my beauty room and, eventually, in my own salon. But my family always had first dibs on my time.

As I said at the beginning, I consider myself lucky to have chosen this industry. My work, however, has always come second to my family. I often wondered how different my career would have been had I not been married and had children. How far up the ladder would I have gone?

These days, girls have a career first, get married and have children much later in life, if they do at all. I was married young by today's standards. I was just twenty when I marched up the aisle. Being an old-fashioned kind of girl, from that day on, my husband and our marriage always came first.

About a year after I was married, a position became available working for Clarins, a major French skin care company. I remember thinking at the interview that I had landed on my feet. Listening to all the great opportunities that came with the position, I knew I was made for this job. It was a perfect fit!

"Of course, we don't want anybody that's likely to get pregnant in the next few years as we'll be investing in them considerably. We require complete commitment." The interviewer said.

"Don't worry, I'm not interested in babies yet", I replied, knowing full well my doctor had my pregnancy test results ready for me to collect later that day.

I wasn't lying at the interview. I wasn't really intending to have babies at the time. Sitting there desperately wanting to get this job, I was just hoping the test would come back negative.

I had barely got home when they called me to say I had got the job and asked me when I could start. They would be organising my training and wanted to know when I was available to travel to Paris. How exciting and glamorous? I couldn't believe my luck.

The next call was with the doctor. I was sure there was a simple explanation for my sore boobs, my sudden hatred of coffee and wanting to puke all day long. It was probably just a bug I had been telling myself. Well, I was wrong!

Now I had received two positive results in one day, and they couldn't have been more different.

I didn't know if I wanted to laugh or cry at the irony. I couldn't possibly take the job knowing as soon as my training was finished a sweet little baby bump would be showing.

The third call that day was to explain to Clarins why I had to change my mind and couldn't accept the position after all. I had mixed feelings as I had missed out on such a brilliant job but was extremely excited to be pregnant.

Over the coming years I had three children and because I always put them first, I swapped and changed jobs on many occasions.

One such occasion was when I worked in a hotel spa. It was practically opposite our house and fitted in well with family needs. Until, that is, I fell in love with the job. My career blossomed; I had become the Assistant Beauty Manageress. I was all set for some amazing opportunities, including the possibility of travelling abroad.

Then one day my eldest, declared, "Mummy, we never see you."

She was right of course, quality time as a family had become scarce. I worked three weekends out of four and every bank holiday. Christmas day was spent at home, but I was back in on Boxing Day. My eldest had made me realise the little job that worked around the family had become a full-on career.

Children grow up fast and there is a limited time when they want to be with you. I wanted to grab this time with open arms, so it was an easy decision and my family won out. Time with my children, who had felt so strongly about me being missing, was of paramount importance to me. So, I gave notice the next day. No travelling for me, for a second time.

The other memorable time I had to give up on a great job for my kids was shortly after my first husband and I split up. My two girls were in senior school and my boy was in his final years of primary school. I was working part time in a lovely salon in Bath.

My two younger children had to stay on their own a couple of hours after school four times a week. They had been doing this for some time while I was still with my husband and it worked well. But after the split they were obviously feeling vulnerable, and typical of children, they expressed this in the only way they knew how, by misbehaving.

One of the first tell-tale signs that things were not as they should have been, was when I came home to candle wax all over the place and a half empty bottle of red wine on the table. On questioning the thirteen-year-old suspect, I found out that she had wanted to set the right ambience for the Ouija Board sessions that she was running for her friends.

The second, and decisive incident, was when I came home from work and found all the windows open in the house and a smell of smoke everywhere. The explanation I received was that they had burnt some chips. I often wonder why kids think that they can pull the wool over mum's eyes. Don't they know we know everything?

It turned out my ten-year-old son, for some reason, had decided to set fire to the paper in the tin bin in his bedroom. On realising that it had got out of hand and he couldn't put it out. He ran to his sister and her friend to sort it out.

The friend, a very gallant lad, picked up the bin with flames as high as his head, and ran out of the house where he put it out with a bucket of water.

Thank God they all got away with no damage to themselves, especially my friend's son. But heeding the warning signs, the next day I handed my notice in so I would be on hand every night after school.

As an aside, that lovely little thirteen-year-old hero is now a married man with two little boys of his own. I'm sure he is a wonderful husband and father. Hopefully, he won't have to put out any fires of his own. Thanks for saving the day George.

I've always believed I've had a successful career for a girl who once thought she would just get married, knock out a couple of kids and have a little job on the side. But I sometimes wonder where I would be now had I been totally dedicated to my career. I could have owned a beautiful and exclusive spa as internationally famous as my talents and abilities would have surely taken me.

But then, would I have had such love and joy from my three amazing children?

Counselling...not my job?

A huge amount of trust develops between people when you give intimate therapies. It's like a magic door opening to reveal every secret the client has. That magic door is called their mouth. With that trust comes the sudden need to tell you all their secrets, worries, problems and dilemmas.

Ask any hairdresser and they will be able to tell you about the surface stuff that's happening in their client's lives. Such things as, where they will be holidaying, what the children are up to, and what their plans are for the weekend. But ask a beauty therapist and they will know the most intimate, closely guarded secrets of all their clients.

Because of the intimate nature of our relationship and the privacy of the therapy room, the secrets flow thick and fast. Some things I've heard have made me laugh my socks off, some have shocked me to the core, and some have even made me cry.

When I touch my clients during a treatment, I often feel their pain. I've always had an intense feeling of wanting to help them. I have always wanted to make things right for them, and take their problems away, so they leave feeling relieved and rejuvenated.

My number one rule for looking after a client is to do amazing treatments and make them feel special. Sometimes all this-takes is a touch on the shoulder or a hug. Listening is another way of helping because often people just want to vent with someone who isn't family or a friend. In our basic training, among the first things we were taught is not to give clients advice. "You are not counsellors." We were told.

Indeed, in the early days of my career I would never have dreamt of giving my opinion to a client. When you first start out you are young and have so little life experience. Who wants a twenty-year-old telling them how to live their life? But as we get older and gain that experience, this rule is not so cut and dried anymore. I found that as I matured, I naturally became better able to help.

Often people really needed that help and there are ways of giving them this without saying, "You should..." I often talked about my own experiences and would tell the client about what others had done under similar circumstances. Obviously, I never mentioned any names. I relied on my instinct and went with my heart, always being careful to be positive and not to overstep the mark.

I once had a lady whom I regularly waxed. She was a single mum raising a daughter on her own. We started chatting as always about children and holidays, etc. But as the months went on, we talked more about her feelings and how she was not satisfied with her life.

She told me about her problematic long distant relationships that were difficult to sustain. Apart from her daughter, she felt unfulfilled in her life. We never talked specifics but during one treatment I just said, "You have to be true to yourself; honest about who you are and what you want from life. You have one life so make it count."

The next time she came for her waxing, she rushed in and said, "I did what you said. I took your advice". Err, this was a worrying moment.

She said excitedly, "I came out!"

She went on to explain how she knew she was gay, and she was hiding it from everyone, hence the long-distance relationships. After our previous conversation, she had decided to tell her family and daughter who she really was. Thankfully, they were all amazing, understanding, and supportive.

The relief was not just huge for her, but for me too. I would never want to give advice and then find it was wrong. She went on to meet a lovely local lady who she settled down with. The last I heard, her daughter was off to university and everything was rosy. You often don't realise you are giving advice; you are just chatting while you work.

A client coming out to me has happened on more than one occasion. I can't help it, people trust me. In one case, a lady just suddenly told me she was gay, and her husband didn't know.

"What do you think I should do?" she asked. Wow! What do you say to that? Thinking on my feet is something I've had to do quite often and that usually means pretending it's all a matter of fact, no big deal, when inside you are screaming, 'OH MY GOD, THIS IS HUGE!'

I don't even remember what I said, but I'm sure it was very reassuring and, hopefully, wise.

Often, the client's timing in spilling the beans about their most intimate secrets can be a little awkward. I was once talking to a lovely doctor who was down on her own from London for a weekend of pampering. We were talking very generally about how men can often be of no help when women are working, running a home, and bringing up children all at the same time.

She was nodding away agreeing with me as I was telling her how a group of my girlfriends had come up with the perfect solution. We would all live together in a woman only commune. Everyone would share the load, look after each other's kids, and do the chores without any nagging. Peace and harmony, as only women can bring.

Just as my head was in close, taking the last few hairs from a very neat bikini line, I finished by saying how useless men could be. She suddenly declared, "That's why I crossed the bridge". I just love being told you are a lesbian while my head is between your legs, waxing your intimate parts.

Always quick on my feet and endeavouring to keep things light, with my head looking at her bits and bobs, I said, "Is it any better the other side?"

She replied, "I'm away for a weekend on my own. So, shall we say it's not without its issues?" We laughed; and what could have been an awkward moment passed by with fun and humour instead of embarrassment.

Don't get me wrong, I'm not saying if you are a lesbian you can't come out to me, it's just that some things I would rather find out looking at your face.

The person on the receiving end of a treatment may feel very self-conscious and it's my job to make them feel comfortable. For example, when you are waxing their intimate areas people can often feel embarrassed. Why wouldn't they; with their legs waving in the air, no pants on or just a paper thong to cover their dignity?

It's my job to try and put them at ease. I do this by telling them funny stories or chatting about everyday stuff. Explaining it's just a normal day's work for me and I've seen it all before. We have a laugh and hopefully the tension disappears.

One time, a gentleman was having laser hair removal treatments. He was having hair removed from everywhere, including his genitals. Previously, his back and chest had been treated. This visit, his penis and balls were being lasered. We knew from the consultation that he was in the process of a gender change. The hair removal was him getting ready for his full operation.

He was naturally feeling vulnerable. Then just to put a cherry on top of his already embarrassed cake. A little dribble of something popped out the top of his penis while I was prepping him for treatment. The poor man was mortified and so embarrassed. Quick as anything I grabbed a tissue and mopped up the mess as if it was just a drop of tea. To ease the tension I asked him, "So will you be having one of those designer vaginas?"

We both laughed and immediately he relaxed as we got on with the job in hand. Being matter of fact and laughing is a great way of dealing with embarrassment.

It's not always funny though. We must learn when to make a comment, and when to shut up. An example of shutting up was when I was treating a lovely lady who had stood by her husband. He had been convicted of having indecent photos of young girls on his computer. She chose to believe her husband's excuse of mistakenly downloading the images. Her family had nothing more to do with her and she lived a very conflicted life.

Like a lot of people, I have strong views on this kind of behaviour. However, the lady was here to have her nails done, and wasn't asking for my opinion. This was a time to remember my basic training and to keep my opinions to myself.

Hair today, gone tomorrow

Waxing looks like the easiest job in the world but ask any new therapist and they dread it. It can be difficult to get this treatment right for a beginner and can be extremely time consuming. My definition of a good waxer is: Being able to remove the hair quickly, efficiently, and cause the least amount of pain for the client. Good training and experience are essential.

There is no doubt it can be a painful treatment to have, but some clients take it in their stride. Often teenagers and young people find waxing extremely painful. But I've also had ladies falling asleep during waxing procedures because they found it so relaxing.

The good news is, the longer you have the area waxed the less pain you feel, because the hair becomes weaker and easier to pull. Different areas are also more uncomfortable than others. The obvious one is the bikini line, but the under arm and top lip can also be very sore. To my mind, the quicker I can get it done, the better for all concerned.

I can knock out a half-leg wax in about ten minutes. And that's with my eyes shut, and one hand tied behind my back. OK, this is a small exaggeration, but you get the point. I've known newbie therapists take over an hour to do this treatment. This is a pain for the therapist, desperately trying to complete the task; as well as the poor client, praying for it to be over.

I wasn't always that quick. As with anything, practise makes perfect. Back when I was a newbie, I used to dread waxing treatments. I can still remember the butterflies I would get before each treatment. Despite my numerous disasters, I decided that I would become the best. Eventually, according to my clients, I was.

I always encourage new therapists and give them lots of tips to make the job easier; always remembering my own butterflies back when I was in their position. When I had my own salon, I would give all new therapists training when they joined me and encouraged them to practise at home. I would say, "Wax everybody and anybody - even the dog."

Some of them couldn't even get the wax from the pot onto the client's leg without dripping it everywhere. Let alone the skill of removing the wax strip with the hair attached. On more than one occasion, I needed to intervene and complete the treatment.

If we don't get it right, clients will return to complain. Areas may have been missed or stubble appear after just a few days. This is caused by the hair being snapped off rather than pulled out. Poor waxing can cause severe in-growing hairs at best, and at worst, it can burn and bruise the skin. These complaints will damage the reputation of a good salon. So, taking the time to train new therapists is a no-brainer.

By far the hardest area to wax is the bikini line (BK line). This has become more difficult over the years as the area required to be waxed became ever more extensive. When I first qualified as a therapist, the area we waxed was the top of the leg where the knicker line ended, and the leg began. Some lady's BK line extends relatively far down the inner leg, but we were never required to venture above the knicker line. Nowadays, there is no place safe from the waxing strip.

I'm sure you all have your own term for your lady parts, but for me it's always been, 'plum'. So, don't get confused and wonder why I'm talking about a fruit in this chapter.

Before I go any further, here's my Guide to BK Waxing Definitions:

Standard means hair removed from the area below and just inside the knicker line. It's also removed from around the top of the leg and the inner thighs.

Extended is the same as standard, but with hair removed a good inch above the knicker line. Also, with your leg in the air like a fairy-tale princess, hair is removed from the outside bum area.

Brazillian is when only a thin strip of hair is left, including on the plum lips. This is known as *the landing strip*. Also removed is everything from your bum. This tends to follow the line of a thong.

Hollywood, this is everything off, including all the hair on your bum. Legs flying all over the place, as you become as naked as the day you were born.

These definitions can mean different things in different countries. For example, Brazillian in Australia tends to be a small area left at the top and everything off below. I always thought this looked like a good impression of a Hitler moustache, whenever they asked me for it.

I have always explained my definitions to all my first-time ladies. We would then discuss shapes of the remaining hair. Would one opt for a thin strip, triangle, or square at the top? Then we had to decide how big the shape would be. Ladies are very particular, and I nearly had to get the ruler out on more than one occasion. I swear sooner or later someone would have asked me for a bush shaped like a bowl of fruit!

Of course, nobody wants a wonky BK line either. I was a perfectionist at getting things exact for my clients. But when it came to my own waxing, it was a different story. I would let all my trainees use me as a guinea pig. My husband would often be left gasping in horror.

"Oh, my Lord, what have you done now?" He would shout. I would be standing there with a crooked landing strip, bald parts where there should have been hair, and long spindly bits where there should have been nothing. Oh, the things I did for my profession!

To give myself a break from the guinea pig sessions, I often begged one of my daughters to come along for a practise session. Given the lack of skills exhibited by some of the young therapists, I'm surprised my girls have not been traumatised for life. But, as the old saying goes, you've got to take the rough with the smooth. They, for their troubles, had lots of lovely treatments.

My youngest daughter didn't mind having a new therapist waxing her bits. But my older daughter was less enthusiastic. Sometimes they both had to be paid off with promises of extra nice treatments. A massage or spray tan normally did the trick. Over the years, both my girls were usually very obliging when I was desperate for a model – thanks chickee's!

You may ask what age is it appropriate to start waxing a bikini line; and what age to perform a Brazillian or Hollywood? This was a big question we had to decide once the more extreme waxing came into fashion. Unlike body piercing or using sun beds, there were no rules or laws. It was left up to the individual salons to decide.

In our salon we decided we would not perform a bikini wax on anyone below senior school age. That meant they had to be at least eleven years old and we also insisted on parental consent. We also decided no Hollywood or Brazillian waxes on anyone below the age of eighteen.

You may think, why wax schoolgirls at all? Well, because they are often embarrassed about their pubic hair when they had to do sports. Remember how cruel girls can be in the changing room? I would also rather wax them than let them loose with a razor on this sensitive area.

The teens were also under pressure to conform to what was the norm. The perceived normal for the younger generation was either everything off, or extraordinarily little hair below. We were always being asked by under-eighteens for Brazillian waxes and Hollywoods. But we always said no.

Unbeknown to me, one incredibly determined teen had managed to book a Hollywood wax with one of my younger therapists.

I encouraged all the therapists who worked for me to call for help, rather than struggle on with a treatment they were having a problem with. "Wendy, I've got in a pickle with this wax, can you help?" The therapist came to tell me one day.

So, I popped into the treatment room and discovered a regular client's fifteen-year-old daughter in the midst of a Hollywood wax. I knew her mother had already told her she couldn't have such an extreme wax. But she had managed to persuade my young therapist to go against the salon rules.

The young girl had extraordinarily strong, thick, curled hair, and was finding the removal unbearably painful. My therapist had struggled with this difficult wax until halfway through. She had indeed got in a right mess. The hair was matted with wax, and areas had been left red raw by continuous attempts at removing the hair.

The young girl was in tears from the pain. I had to take over and remove the matted wax and tidy her up the best I could. I refused to remove any more hair so she would not be having her intended Hollywood. She didn't complain because she was in so much pain anyway. She just wanted the job done as quickly as possible and get out of there. This was a little karma I think for going behind her mum's back.

The young girl was rather sheepish; especially when I told her I needed to let her mum know what had happened. Luckily, the lady was a good client of mine and she took it well.

I had strong words with all my therapists after this and made sure they understood our policy concerning under-eighteen's bikini waxing.

Another thing I had to contend with was sorting out dodgy Brazillians and Hollywoods done by other salons. They would be left unfinished, because the therapist didn't have the experience to do the job proficiently.

We regularly had clients come straight from another salon, with their plum lips stuck together from wax left behind. Sometimes they would be crying in pain and telling war stories about how they had been lying on a couch for far too long with the therapist sweating in panic and them writhing in agony.

Literally traumatised by previous waxing, they would arrive with stories of wax pots being balance between their legs. They told us of how vulnerable and terrified they had felt for fear of the wax spilling and burning them. I never told these distressed clients of the horror stories I had heard where that had actually happened, causing burns and blisters.

There were tales of therapists continually waxing the same area over and over again, trying to remove the hair. But all they were doing was ripping the skin from this delicate area. A wax pot in the hands of an unqualified or inexperienced therapist can be a dangerous weapon.

It's also astonishing how many therapists blame everything else except themselves for a bad job. One poor client was told that she was too skinny to have the hair removed from the top of her inner thigh. How unbelievably rude to call someone skinny! And on this occasion, it really upset the client as she was extremely conscious of her weight.

Having said that, removing hair from the very top of the inner thigh can be difficult. You must be extremely careful as the skin in this area can bruise easily. It's particularly important to have the leg in the right position. And that position does depend on the weight and shape of the client, as well as how flexible they are. Extremely slim ladies and ladies on the larger size are always more difficult to wax.

It was always so important to me to do a professional job. And part of that was client positioning. You need to be assertive and get your client in some peculiar positions. It's all about getting the job done properly. I've never had a problem with this. Determined and focused; my aim was a quick, efficient, and thorough result. If that meant getting legs akimbo or the client helping by stretching her skin, so be it.

Different size ladies and different ages all mean you must change the way you position each client. You cannot be a wall flower and perform this type of treatment. It's head down and get stuck in. In the end, nobody ever minded when they were looking in the mirror at their perfect BK line.

As I've already mentioned, you cannot expect some poor newbie therapist to come along and do an extreme bikini wax. They are not even trained at college to do Brazillian or Hollywood waxes. They may have only ever seen a demonstration of it. Yet silly salon owners and managers will simply throw these poor girls in at the deep end. Then they wonder why the girl gets in a mess and the clients keep complaining.

In the past I've offered to teach intimate waxing in colleges. But they have always refused my offer, with the excuse that this type of waxing throws up all kinds of safeguarding issues. Yet, they are perfectly willing to throw these girls out into the workplace with no idea of what they are facing and call them qualified.

I loved waxing, and especially enjoyed Brazilian and Hollywood waxes as they were always a challenge. Unfortunately, some clients were not always a pleasure to treat, due to their personal hygiene.

There were some ladies that really didn't wash enough down below. Thank goodness they were few and far between. Even an offer of a baby wipe, prior to a treatment, was not enough to stop the room needing some serious air freshening before the next client. I am lucky my sense of smell has always been bad, so I often didn't notice myself. But when the people in the shop next door start complaining, you know there's a problem. Only joking! It was never really that bad.

If I did smell something unpleasant, it would have to be extremely strong. Everybody would know the drill: doors open, discreet spraying of air freshener throughout, no flapping or giggling, business as usual.

Often accompanying the smell would be discharge. I told you it wasn't a glamorous job, didn't I? Some discharge is perfectly normal, and it's all part of the human body working efficiently. The normal, everyday stuff is not unpleasant, just part of the job and completely acceptable.

However, when its sticky, yellow, smelly stuff oozing out all over the place we've crossed into horror movie territory. This was most definitely the time to stop the treatment. In fact, stop the world!

Some people need some health and hygiene guidance. Some, lots of understanding and acceptance. Others just needed to be guided to another salon tout de suite.

I would explain to the client that they had an infection and needed to go and see the doctor. Some younger girls didn't realise this wasn't the norm; and these were the times for an understanding and guiding hand. But I could never really understand the older ladies. You would have thought that they had enough life experience to recognise when they had a problem that required a doctor, or over-the-counter medication. The worst for me were the clients who had simply been unclean for so long, that they now had a nasty discharge to prove it.

In cases of abnormal discharge, we would never carry out the treatment. We would refer them to a doctor and tell them to come back when everything was sorted. If they were just unclean, we would grit our teeth (and our nose) and get on with it. If they were very smelly, we would try our hardest not to book them in again. In these cases, we would always be 'too busy' to fit them in. Sometimes, they would sneak under the *smelly radar*, and we would be left dreading it as we walked them to the treatment room.

Some of the ladies had a problem with hygiene because of mental health issues. I would always book these clients in with me. Firstly, because my sense of smell was so bad and secondly, because I felt I was helping them. At the end of the day, it's all about looking after people, isn't it? My clients as well as my therapists!

Talking of discharge, I used to really appreciate the clients who would come screeching into the salon five minutes after having sex. Show some respect and have a wash first please.

You may also want to remember; your sex life is not something I want to discuss while waxing your plum. Chat about everyday stuff: weather, children, or the latest fashions, but never sex.

Most memorable, was the girl getting her first Hollywood because her boyfriend was getting his *Brown Wings* that night. I had to ask my young therapists what that meant. All the girls in the salon thought it was hysterical that I didn't know. That one kept them amused for a whole week.

If you are all wondering what that means? I'm not going to tell you; it's not that kind of book. Best you Google it.

Then there was the older lady having her second Hollywood. She proudly started discussing how I had changed her sex life. Apparently, her older husband was like a new man and she wished she had had the lot off years ago. Though it was kind of sweet, I still didn't want to hear it with my hands on the lips of her plum.

I also remember the very odd young girl that spent the whole time screaming in an erotic way every time I ripped her hair out. I was thinking, "Is she just in pain or is she getting off on this?"

All was revealed when she declared she was an artist who took moulds of her vagina and made sculptures out of them. She went on to say, "I love pain. When you finish this, I'm putting my rough jeans on with no underwear, jumping on the back of my boyfriend's bike and riding until I'm sore."

After she left, I told the salon owner and the receptionist never to book her in with me again. The owner wasn't best pleased, as she was thinking of losing the money. But her mind soon changed when I suggested she should carry out the treatment herself next time.

Over the years, I also had young couples arrive wanting the boyfriend to watch the waxing session. An unequivocal, "No!" was always my answer. Obviously, I was never rude and always tried to be diplomatic. Sometimes, the boyfriend would beg, but there was no way I was going to be part of their foreplay.

You learn with age, and through experience, how to be firm. After all, you have the right to feel just as comfortable as the client does. There is nothing worse than feeling embarrassed, or humiliated while performing such an intimate treatment.

While I was working in the spa in particular, I had my fair share of uncomfortable and inappropriate moments.

It's very unpleasant knowing someone is paying to get off on you. I even know of one poor therapist who had a client that got so excited during the treatment that she actually had an orgasm.

Companies sometimes introduce new gadgets to help with waxing. Some are better than others. A waxing rep once produced a long, oval, plastic cup from her bag. She declared, "It comes in pink, pale blue, mint green and it's for intimate waxing. The client inserts it between the lips of her vagina, covering the clitoris area."

The idea was to protect the area and the client's modesty. It was reusable, so after the treatment the client would wash it, take it home and return with it the next time.

I found it an amusing and interesting concept. Though, I did wonder about the one-size-fits-all approach. Before committing to buying a job lot, I took a sample and asked my regular clients what they thought of the idea.

"Protect what modesty? We leave that at the door!" They said. They wanted the treatment done and dusted as quickly as possible without fumbling about with this funny plastic contraption. And nobody wanted to take it home and wash it.

These little boat-like contraptions didn't take off in our salon, but I do understand they are still on sale on the internet if you fancy trying one out.

Colouring the pubic area was another very short-lived fad. Colours available included bright green, pink, blue and purple. It never took off in the main, which I had mixed feelings about. On the one hand, can you imagine all the different disasters that could happen; with colours going wrong and clients complaining about their multi-coloured plums? On the other hand, think of the growth line every six weeks. That would have been a great little earner, touching up the roots.

As a foot note: I really enjoyed waxing and especially the bikini line. 99% of my clients were wonderful and appreciated my skills. They would often travel many miles rather than have a poor wax. I appreciated you all!

Adorn my body

For hundreds and thousands of years we have adorned our bodies in lots of different ways. Cavemen were known to paint their bodies for rituals, and they wore jewellery made from bones. To this day we still feel the need to decorate our bodies in the name of beauty.

Fads come and go. Nowadays, it's celebrities who often start a trend. One vintage watch worn by someone famous, and suddenly everyone wants one. The Only Way is Essex was a catalyst for the Vajazzel. The treatment was known as Vajazzling and was the application of shimmering gems to the recently waxed bikini area.

You could buy pre-made designs or apply individual gems to make your own. It was great fun and brought out our artistic sides. As usual, I was the guinea pig when we first introduced this treatment into the salon.

I had a lovely sparkling butterfly positioned just below my hip bone. But because I swam four times a week, pulling my trousers on and off, it didn't take long for me to start losing my Vajazzel.

A couple of weeks after the application of my beautiful butterfly I was stripping off ready to go for a swim. Imagine a whole changing room full of goggle-eyed women staring at, what can only be described as, a half-eaten moth. How embarrassing!

These were all the rage for everyone from teens to ladies in their sixty's. Everyone seemed to want a Vajazzel. Personally, I thought they looked more attractive on smooth young skin, rather than older flabby, skin.

But one older lady said, "I want to celebrate my large, stretch-marked stomach. I earned it and have three beautiful children to prove it." So, I promptly vajazelled the length of her caesarean scar with coloured diamonds.

One Saturday we had five Vajazzlings booked in, and we were all gob-smacked when a group of twenty-something men walked in. It was a stag do, and they all wanted a little bit of bling to show off later in the evening. We had great fun with the lads applying these gemstones extremely low on their hip bones. One of the therapists even designed a cute, free-hand bunny. They were all trying to get her to meet up with them later to so say, give her credit for her artwork.

As the bikini line got higher, so the number of intimate piercings and tattoos in this area increased. Suddenly every area of the body was now beautified.

Before we knew it, the clit ring had appeared. Whenever I saw that little ring it made me cringe. I couldn't get out of my head the pain of having it pierced in the first place, or the thought of accidently getting it caught in your zipper.

It intruded on the Hollywood Wax too. The ring needed to be kept out of the way, for fear of accidentally ripping it out with the waxing strip. Thank God this never happened to me. I have, however, heard about it happening to other therapists. I bet you are cringing now.

Tattoos were also invading my workspace and becoming ever more popular on females. I completely understand different people liking different things but, my goodness, I've seen some dodgy inking.

There's the usual array of dolphins, flowers, and butterflies. But there are also some bizarre tats out there. The less attractive ones I recall are snakes looping down towards the plum, or the phrase, *get it here*, situated on the pubic bone. Luckily, they were confined to the intimate area and not on full display.

I've seen tattoos that were hard to decipher, such as the lady who had Chinese lettering, which looked like a child had drawn a black aeroplane in a pre-school class. There were messy black blobs on ladies that had had tats done when they were still kids. These were shoddy work from tattoo butchers, who were willing to ink under eighteens.

I don't want to sound like 'Grandma Wendy'. I have a tattoo, which I love. I know tattoos are popular and I'm not against them. It's just that I've seen so many bad ones over the years and have come across so many people that wished they'd never had them done. But they aren't all bad, are they?

One of my regular clients, a stunning young woman, had the most elaborate tats I've ever seen. Flowers in all kinds of colours were climbing from her ankle, round her legs, up the side of her thighs, and onto her tummy. There were exotic Polynesian birds on her arms, and she even had plans to add more tattoos. She was a walking piece of art, and it suited her style.

She was a pretty girl anyway without the tats. But with the inking it made her stand out in any crowd. The age-old question is… what will they look like when she gets older, when her skin becomes wrinkled and inevitably loses its elasticity? Will her beautiful array of exotic flowers look like an abandoned garden full of weeds?

Probably not! This beautiful, stylish girl will probably find some way of staying eternally young; poll dancing into her seventies, with her wilted garden still being a beautiful, artistic statement.

When I first started in this profession, a therapist would never have been seen with tattoos. You just wouldn't have got a job, particularly in any kind of luxury spa. The same went for piercings, especially on the face. But nowadays these tattoos and piercings have become acceptable everywhere. In some salons, having an array of this sort of thing is essential for their trendy image.

One day, a man turned up on our doorstep asking for work experience. He wasn't planning on becoming just a masseur but a full-on beauty therapist. He planned to qualify for manicures, pedicures, and everything else in between. This was an unusual choice of profession for a man. He explained, he saw his future in the up and coming male market.

Back then we were always taking on potential therapists so they could gain experience in a working salon. As well as learning about the everyday running of a salon, they would also sit in on some treatments, though never the intimate ones.

He being a man was no problem. I did, however, have a problem with all the tattoos covering his hands and arms; especially as they looked harsh and aggressive. I knew my older ladies wouldn't like this and would see it as offensive.

Clients were always my priority. Keeping them happy is the most important part of running a successful business. So, I wished the chap good luck in his future career and sent him on his way.

Piercings were also a problem and even if they were taken out for work, the therapists were still left with unsightly holes. Some potentially good therapists were sent on their way because there were too many holes in their body that weren't there when they were born.

Some client piercings could be problematic during their treatments. During a facial, nose piercings got in the way of a relaxing massage. Even if the stud was removed for the treatment, you were constantly trying to get stubborn product out of the hole. I have already mentioned the annoying clitoris ring, which was always in the way unless it was taken out for the treatment.

Then came dermal piercing. This type of piercing has no exit hole. It's a single-point, surface piercing. It looks like you have a jewel or stone in your skin. It's a little like it's been stamped in. Unlike traditional piercings you don't take them in and out. You will often see them in the centre of the collar bone, normally a small stone sitting in the skin. They can, however, be anywhere on the body.

In my opinion the odd one can look very pretty. But like everything else, some people can go a little over the top.

Working around these types of piercings can be a bit of a nuisance. One client booked a back massage, and when I removed the towel, revealed a row of little diamonds down her spine. There must have been at least ten of the little devils. It was a nightmare trying to perform a flowing massage, as I had to keep avoiding the slightly protruding stones.

During another facial the client had these little piercings running down the side of her neck, slowly snaking around to her spine. My hands just couldn't avoid them, and it made the massage exceedingly difficult for me and not as satisfying for her.

My wonderful massage is the best part of any treatment, and both these ladies missed out.

The way we decorate ourselves has become ever more extreme over the years. The things we do to our bodies all in the interest of, what we perceive as, beauty.

To spa or not to spa?

Originally a spa would be found in cities or towns with natural beneficial springs. There are lots of famous spa towns in the UK, such as Bath, Cheltenham, or Leamington Spa.

Bathing in natural spring waters for healing benefits has been well documented for thousands of years. The Romans spring to mind when we think of bathing in therapeutic waters and they are thought to have introduced them when they invaded Britain. However, the Saxons had been soaking themselves in hot spring waters for cleanliness and relaxation way before the Romans arrived in Britain.

Nowadays, spa days are offered everywhere and are a great way for any hotel to earn extra money. High end, luxury, or bargain basement, it's a treat and a tonic. A relaxing day lying around the pool while waiting for your massage appointment is a slice of heaven. Add to this a couple of girlfriends and lunch with a glass of bubbly and you've got paradise.

Tapping into this luxury environment, the word, *spa* on a body product adds perceived value. A spa product added to your bath water makes you feel much more pampered than the supermarket bubble bath. If it's a product you purchased during your spa day, the aroma will take you back to that feeling of relaxation and pampering. I think that's well worth the high price tag, don't you?

My days working in a spa came unexpectedly. I was fed up with one of my working-from-home stints and was finding it rather lonely. My children were now at school and I wanted to go out to work rather than merely climb the stairs to my treatment room. Just across the road from me was a country hotel with a spa and it was advertising for a therapist.

The nearest town to me was eight miles in any direction, so this would be the perfect job. I could ride to work on my pushbike and was only two minutes from school at pick up time. Applying for this job was originally only for convenience; but ended up being some of the best days of my career. As well as being so much fun, it was also an education in treatments, products, and life experience.

This was no ordinary hotel. It was part of the Relais & Châteaux group and it even had its own equestrian centre. This was the crème de la crème of hotels, set in beautiful grounds in the English countryside. The rich and famous would pop in from all over the world. They would all overindulge in wine, food, and pampering treatments. Nothing was too much for the guests, and high-quality service was everything.

Suddenly, I was now charging seventy pounds for a body massage, rather than twenty. Getting my head around this took some time. I was told to remember they are not just paying for the treatment, but for the luxurious environment as well.

During my first two months I didn't know what had hit me and have never worked so hard in my life. Originally employed on an eight-hour contract, I did twice these hours. I worked most weekends too as this was the busiest times.

For the first few months, during my probationary period, I wasn't trained in the advanced treatments or product houses. So, manicures, pedicures, and massage were my usual treatments. A full body massage tended to be the treatment of choice for most guests.

These were a one-hour appointment and guests were booked in on the hour every hour. I began my day at ten or eleven in the morning. And there were appointments booked back to back for eight solid hours, except for my half-hour lunch.

When my guests arrived, I would welcome them and take them upstairs to one of the beautiful treatment rooms. A consultation followed, with an explanation of the treatment and how to get ready. Then I would leave them for a couple of minutes while they undressed and got comfortable on the couch.

I would normally linger outside the room, but soon learnt that if you left them for five minutes this could be a good opportunity to run downstairs and take a swig of cold coffee. When you were feeling exhausted on a long day and hadn't had a drink for hours, a caffeine hit was essential.

A knock on the door to check the client was ready and in I went, ready to start the treatment. Five minutes before the end of the hour I would tell them to relax for a few minutes, and then they could get dressed and come downstairs to the reception room. I would then run downstairs and grab a glass of water ready for them. By this time, my next client would have arrived so I would need to greet them and offer them a glass of water too. I would then dash back upstairs, change the towels, and prepare the room ready to bring the next person up.

I did this routine every hour most days. If we were lucky, there would be a receptionist, who would bill the treatments to the room on the computer. But most days you had to fit this into the day, as well. On busy days you just hoped there was no guest waiting in reception, browsing at products, or waiting for advice. This would be yet another thing to fit into your hectic day.

Clients would arrive one after the other and, of course, by the end of the morning you were inevitably running behind time. This always ate into your lunch break. On a good day, I would have twenty minutes for lunch. On a bad one, it was ten minutes. On a nightmare day it was just a bite here and there of a cold meal. We ran on adrenalin, not food.

Of course, this well-oiled machine would often come unstuck. I would be waiting in reception for the client to come down, only for them not to appear. Up those steps I would trot again, only to find them snoring on the couch. I told you I was good!

Sometimes, I would have to return to the room a couple of times to wake them up. I soon learnt, you needed to give the sleepers a good shake, to make sure they had fully come around, before leaving the room.

On one occasion I remember a different type of sleeper all together. A famous rock star came over late in the day for a massage. After the treatment he failed to come down, so we assumed he was a sleeper. However, on returning to the room he couldn't be woken up for love nor money.

He was still breathing but he had passed out cold. We were even starting to think about calling an ambulance, as two of us were vigorously trying to shake him awake. Just as we were starting to panic, he came round.

Finally, after getting dressed he arrived back in reception. It soon became obvious why he had taken so long to come round. He was completely out of it on drugs or alcohol, or maybe both. I suspect he didn't even register having the treatment, although he did leave a hefty tip.

I would come home after a day's work and fall asleep in the chair before I had even contemplated a cup of tea or a glass of wine. The full body massages, coupled with the stairs, made me drop a stone in weight just like that. I could eat whatever I liked. It was an instant diet and remained so the whole time I worked there. After about two months though I finally got used to the work and no longer felt exhausted.

I fell in love with the hotel and the job within two weeks. I've always loved my work, but I really loved this job. The opulence, the luxury, the rich and the famous, I loved it all. I felt part of something special and I would say that most of the staff who worked in the hotel felt the same.

In Disney's *Beauty and the Beast* there is a song called *Be Our Guest*. It's about being at your guest's beck and call, serving them and making everything perfect - and this was how I felt. I wanted to give our guests a wonderful pampering experience. From the reviews that people left I know that we really did achieve this.

There was also a prestige in the local village about the hotel. I was originally known as a mum who carried out a few beauty treatments at home. Now, I worked in the spa and treated the rich and famous. Suddenly everyone wanted to know me. I couldn't walk to the local shop without being asked about work. Who had I treated? Had anyone famous been in?

I especially, loved the spa for showing me how the other half lived. The guests loved to share their stories of their good fortune. One regular would tell me how every year or two she would go to the Bentley showroom, drink champagne, and eat canapés. All while she chose colours for the interior of her new car and all the extras she wanted. On one visit, she gladly took my son to the car park and showed him her new Bentley. My little boy loved cars and it made his week. I was always so grateful to her for that.

I also remember the husband who rented the whole hotel for a party weekend for his wife's fortieth birthday. All the guests were given free treatments. It was February at the time, and everyone had a personalised brolly just in case it rained. He arranged for them all to travel from the hotel in old-fashioned buses, to take a tour of Bath. Then they were taken to hire Georgian costumes to wear at the ball that night back at the hotel.

It was to be an elaborate affair with lots of food, wine, and dancing. Of course, we would be prepping all the ladies; painting their fingernails and applying their make-up. All this was not that unusual for this type of luxury hotel. The husband had also arranged for an incredibly famous actor to perform a unique piece for his wife. The actor was a regular on British television at the time. Goodness knows how much he charged for such an intimate event.

The weekend was finished off with an impressive BBQ. The whole entourage departed, and there was one incredibly happy wife. Although one thing that struck me about the entire occasion was that whenever I saw the husband, he always had headphones on and a microphone to his mouth. It seemed throughout all this wonderful party and elaborate weekend that he was never fully present, as work was always with him.

Another, family springs to mind for having it all. They came each year to spend Christmas at the hotel. None of us ever minded working at this magical time. The place was always made to look like a country manner from a Charles Dickens novel. There were open fires in every room, chocolates, and nuts on every table. The hotel even supplied stockings for every guest on Christmas morning, no matter what their age.

This family was very well off. They lived in London, and the man was big in finance. They had six children ranging in age from pre-school to teenagers. The lady was rather stunning and looked immaculate in her simple designer outfits. All the kids were good looking and polite. They looked like a perfect TV land family.

It was always a commotion when they arrived on Christmas Eve. We would all rush to look at the presents that would arrive before them in a transit van. The whole reception area would be strewn with beautifully wrapped up presents. Yet, still sitting proudly in their original designer labelled shopping bags: Gucci, Emporio Armani, Ralph Lauren for the adults and older children. And Hamley's bags, big and small, ready for the little ones.

It really was an extraordinary sight. Rumour had it they even had an extra room booked just to store the presents. It was Christmas indulgence at its best.

The whole family would take in the beautiful countryside while out horse riding or on push bikes. They would all swim in the beautiful indoor pool, before sitting in front of one of the huge, open fires with tea and yummy homemade Christmas confectionary. The husband and wife would be in one of the beauty rooms daily (sometimes twice) indulging in wonderful treatments. Even the teenagers were treated to the odd massage or facial. It seemed like an idyllic life, but things are not always what they seem.

The last I heard, the man was waiting to go to trial and fraud was the rumour. I don't know if he was innocent or guilty or what became of him. But I never heard of them returning for their Christmas indulgences again. This is just another example of looking at the wrapping paper and thinking, *how perfect*. Only to find things were not quite what you thought they were beneath the pretty packaging.

I especially loved Christmas. Though it was an exhausting time to work, and I spent far too much time away from my children. But it was like stepping into a book, and I was making someone's fairy tale real. I can still remember the smell of the place. It didn't just look like Christmas, it smelled like it too! The smell of pine needles and mulled spices drifted around every corner. But despite the wonder of it all, I was always happy to come home to my own real-life fairy tale. My simple life with my three children in my little three-bed terrace.

I saw this type of opulence all the time over my years of working in the spa. But seeing how the other half lived, I was never envious. Yes, they could afford the best of everything. But there was often a price to pay.

In fact, I remember one wealthy lady telling me that she envied *my* life. She was much better off financially than me, to say the least. But she said she would have loved the opportunity to live in the countryside as I did - rather than having to live in London, where her children had no freedom. To have a husband that came home every night - rather than her man having to live half the year in another country for tax purposes. Money isn't the be all and end all, is it?

Massage... Any extras?

Do some people think my work is sexual? Absolutely!

Mention the word massage at a party and watch the men snigger and nudge their mates. They are suddenly transported back to their teenage years in the boy's changing room.

OK, there is something very personal about touching someone. Running your hands over their body and gently caressing them is very relaxing and, of course, it can be sensual. It can also make you feel cosseted and protected, just like when your mother rubbed your back or soothed your brow. It's the feeling of someone wanting to take away your worries, of caring for you and wanting to make you feel wonderful. All of that is a long way away from being sexual though.

As a massage therapist you can't give out a sexual vibe, especially when you're treating a man. It's important to be professional and friendly without being flirtatious. We sometimes have men that only see massage as sexual. That was especially true years ago when I first started in the industry. Nowadays, more men use massage regularly to de-stress, and thankfully, it has lost some of its sexual connotations.

I'm comfortable massaging male clients, but this has come through experience - good and bad. I would, however, feel uncomfortable massaging a male friend or family member. I set my own comfort zone and work within it.

Despite massage having lost a lot of its sexual overtones, it remains a sensual treatment. Some men avoid massage because it is outside of their comfort zone.

There was a nice man who was staying with his wife at the exclusive hotel. I remember they were both rather young and were a little like fish out of water. I think they were there for an anniversary, treating themselves.

The wife had several treatments, clearly enjoyed them, and wanted her husband to join in the relaxing experience. "Have a massage, I want you to relax", she kept saying. She badgered him so much he agreed to have his first ever massage. So, she booked him a full body treatment.

He was rather nervous when I took him upstairs to the beauty room. Realising this, I tried to put him at ease. I chatted to him while I made sure he knew what to expect from the treatment. I explained everything thoroughly, wanting him to not feel anxious about the procedure.

I remember it was summertime, so the windows were open, the fresh country air was wafting lazily into the room and soft music was playing as we began. As was usual he was lying face-down on the couch. I began with a relaxing scalp massage, moving onto firmer movements on his back.

I spent about twenty minutes on his back then moved onto his legs. He was a little fidgety and it was obvious he wasn't relaxing, so I asked if the pressure was OK. "Was he too cold or too warm?"

"Everything's fine." He said, even though it clearly wasn't.

All became apparent when it was time for him to turn over. I said, "I'll hold the towels up and you turn over. Then I'll place the towel on top as you lie on your back." We look away at this point, and I swear I heard him say, "Oh shit!'', as he turned over.

As I let the towel fall on him… his penis was so erect that there was a tent made by the towel. Suddenly, it was all too obvious why he was not enjoying the massage.

"I'm so sorry." He said miserably, "I knew this may happen. I didn't want a massage, but my wife persuaded me."

I felt embarrassed for him. It's true what they say, they really do have a mind of their own!

I assured him these things happen all the time (not that often). I suggested we stop the treatment, which he gratefully agreed to. I left him to get dressed and told him I wouldn't charge him for the massage. Just before I left the room, I advised him that next time his wife insisted he had a treatment, maybe a pedicure would be preferable… and just hoped he didn't have a foot fetish.

This was clearly a nice young man who could not handle the sensuality of a massage. But there is another type of man who is not so pleasant. This type gets their kicks from making the therapist feel uncomfortable, and clearly, they are having a massage for sexual gratification. Though massage is therapeutic there will always be some who come purely to get their rocks off.

I once had a beautiful young therapist working for me in the spa. She really was a stunning girl. But she was also highly professional and extremely intent on her clients having the best possible treatment. I was Deputy Manageress at the time and this girl came to me one Sunday morning worried and upset.

"Wendy, I have this man booked in with me for his third full-body massage in less than twenty-four hours, and he's requested me each time." This was not that unusual as clients staying in the hotel for the weekend often had a daily massage.

But she went on to say, "He makes me feel cheap. He wants all the towels off and wants me to spend most of my time on his upper legs. He asks me personal questions and he gives me a twenty-pound tip every time. I think he's getting aroused."

I've always felt protective over the young girls who worked for me. I helped them to become excellent therapists, in return they gave me loyalty and hard work. I would never expect them to do a treatment that made them feel uncomfortable. So, I immediately swapped clients with her.

Before the man came over, I prepared the room. I purposely left the window open so the cold November chill would cool the room. The man came over and I explained there had been a mistake with the bookings and I would be doing his massage. As I walked him to the room, I asked him lots of questions about his family and made a point of talking about his wife, with whom he was staying at the hotel.

I explained the treatment, told him how to get ready, and left him for five minutes, as was the norm. Knocking on the door and coming back into the room it was clear he had removed his under clothing, (my instructions had been to leave them on), and his towel was placed half on and half off his body. I immediately put the towel fully over him, explaining how important it was to keep the muscles warm during a massage. Not long into the massage he started to complain about being too hot and wanted me to remove the large towel, suggesting I cover him with a small one.

"No, no!" I said. "It's awfully bad for the muscles to be uncovered during a massage. If you're too warm, we'll open the window." As I was opening the window, I could see the last of the frost and snow on the ground. It was damn cold.

Normally I never talk during a massage because I want my client to drift into another world and feel deeply relaxed. But in this case, I wanted his mind on subjects that wouldn't arouse him. So, I talked about his children, grandchildren, and his wife. How was she enjoying her stay? Where was she now? Had they been shopping in the city yet?

Then he declared that he wanted me to spend most of the treatment on his inner thighs and top of his legs. Now, this area is an erogenous zone and not an area we usually spend any length of time on during a massage. It's very much an area, especially on a man, where only certain movements would be performed.

I told him this would be terribly bad and would over-stimulate the muscles. I suggested that some hacking movements would stimulate the area if he had tense muscles. This is a movement that is not sexual in any way. I chopped away at his inner thighs to my heart's content. Then promptly turned my attention back to all the subjects I could think of that would not give him any kind of erotic thoughts.

He still had a good massage - just not the kind he wanted!

After the one-hour treatment he came to reception and we charged the cost to his room. Just before he left to go back to the main hotel, I was surprised that he turned back to give me a tip. It was only two pounds. Which was a little less than the twenty pounds he had given the younger therapist on each of his treatments with her.

I was satisfied I had put him in his place, protected my therapist from a nasty little predator and got a tip for my trouble. But it didn't take long for word to get round the beauty rooms, the spa, and the rest of the hotel. She was worth twenty pounds and I was only worth two. Boy, did I get some ribbing for that one.

In my original interview for the spa position, one of the first questions asked was… "Do you have experience massaging men?"

I knew if I wanted the job, I would have to sound self-assured and confident about this. But the truth was, I had only done a couple of back massages on a few clients' husbands. I thought, the job would mean I would massage a just few men, which wouldn't have been much of a problem. But OMG! I was not prepared for just how many men I would be treating in the spa.

This was the nineties and the Metrosexual man was appearing everywhere. Suddenly, the chemists were full of male anti-aging moisturisers and body creams. Businessmen, especially those down from London, didn't think twice about having a de-stressing massage and a facial. Half my clientele was suddenly male.

I soon started harping on about how big the male industry would become in the next ten years. I should have put a bet on that one too.

In the years that followed, I often talked about opening my own male-only salon. This didn't ever happen, mainly because, although I didn't mind treating men, I just didn't like it as much as treating my ladies.

Around half the clients at weekends in the spa were men. Often this would be one half of a couple. Most of them I was happy to treat but there was a certain type that I dreaded.

It was the *hairy man*!

Now, I'm not talking about the stuff that grows on the top of your head, but the stuff all over the body. Some men are just so hairy, with coarse hair on their backs, legs, arms and basically, everywhere.

Some guys would walk through the door and you could tell they had lots of body hair straight away. The hair would be protruding out of their shirt sleeves or popping out of the top of their T shirts. This was OK because you could gear yourself up for a *hairy man* massage.

It was the unexpected that got me. The blonde, blue-eyed chap or the ginger guy who walked in and I would think,

"Great, it's a smooth body." Only to return to the room to pull back the towel and reveal a man that looked like he had just jumped out of the trees. No offence.

You see, when you are constantly rubbing coarse hair, it really irritates your hands and makes them red and sore. For me it was like someone scraping their nails down a blackboard. After all my years massaging it still makes me cringe. With men that were exceptionally hairy you needed to massage with care, otherwise the hair would get knotted up. As careful as you were, I swear, sometimes I needed a comb to detangle the hair before they left the room.

Often, the men would book for a sports massage just because it sounded manly. They thought Swedish massage would be too girly for them. We would always ask them what they wanted from the treatment. Most of the time it was relaxation, so would recommend a Swedish, rather than a sport, massage. We would have to reassure them that this could still be a firm massage as well as relaxing.

Some men who had regular massages elsewhere would arrive at the spa, and upon seeing me, would give me, *The Look*.

The Look meant they were thinking, "look how tiny this bird is, she'll never be strong enough to sort my muscles out. I'm going to have a crap massage."

Now as I said, I'm only five-foot two inches, and I probably weighed about seven and a half stone back then. So, I did look like I wouldn't be able to give a firm massage. But I could, and I loved to prove these guys wrong. If only I had a penny for every time these men would say, in disbelief, after a few minutes of massage... "You have very strong hands for someone so small."

Then, there were the rugby players and gym bunnies. Oh boy! They were really hard work for me. It would be like trying to manipulate rocks instead of muscles. Your heart would sink if you had a muscle man booked in at the end of the day when you were feeling totally knackered.

Then there was the worst scenario of all for me. The big hairy, muscle man walks in. You are already knackered and it's your last appointment. And he gives you *The Look,* and you think, "Shit! He's giving me T*he Look*, now I'm going to have to prove him wrong".

Joking aside, throughout my career I tried to give all my clients the best possible treatment. Whether it was first thing in the morning or last thing on a late night. This meant hairy muscle man, who gave me *The Look*, got the best massage he had probably ever had. I would get sore hands and often went home doubly knackered, but everybody got the best from me.

I paid for it all later with Carpel Tunnel Syndrome, and a little premature arthritis – but it was worth it!

As a rule, men and women would be told to take everything off, apart from their pants. Americans and others that were used to massage would take everything off. That's how they were massaged elsewhere, so that's how they intended to be massaged with us. Now, to me, in treatment terms, I see a naked body very much anatomically. But there was a sound reason for the pants-on rule in the male massage.

You see, it kept everything nicely in place and out of the way. The problem was that once the pants were off the 'rabbit' would escape and you never knew where the damn thing would pop up.

"I touched it!" I would shout inside my own head, while screwing up my nose. I would be happily massaging away, not too close to the top of the leg or inner thigh, when suddenly, it would be limply lying there, and I would brush against it.

"Oh shit", you would think, contemplating why it was hanging so low. I always made myself believe the client hadn't noticed, and just carried on as though nothing had happened. Although I'm sure they always did.

My boss and I had a regular client we shared. We alternated late nights, so his weekly massage was with one or other of us. He was an older, charming man and we got to know him well. He was a little flirtatious but not in any inappropriate way. He enjoyed relaxing, and once on the couch he was very chilled out and enjoyed his regular massage.

But he had this game he would play. It was initially an unintentional game, but in the end, planned. He liked to be massaged naked, and because he was a regular, we accepted this. He also liked to have a chat and catch-up each time we saw him. He would chat away to us as we went upstairs and then start undressing while still nattering. First of all, it was just shoes and socks and then we realised what the game was.

He was trying to keep us chatting so he could get butt-naked in front of us before we had a chance to get out the room. We would laugh so much about the lengths he went to for us to catch a glimpse of his willy. He got faster and faster at undressing, but we got even faster at leaving the room.

We always found him harmless and amusing rather than predatory. He never actually caused us any problems or offence.

Because you treated so many men, you soon learnt how to handle all varieties. The nice man mentioned above had a sense of humour. There were also the flirtatious types, the embarrassed, and the shockers, to name a few. We were all surprisingly good at judging the type and how to handle them. Being aware of the type before placing your hands on someone was especially advantageous in handling the pervy ones.

Sometimes a perv can catch you out though. Your internal alarm bell doesn't sound in time, or you are just too busy to listen to it.

For example, there was the very good-looking, Jack-the-lad down from London. I'll call him Mr Cockney. He was staying in the hotel for the weekend and had a few treatments booked.

On the Saturday afternoon he had a back massage booked with me. He was pretty chatty while I was massaging him, and we talked about me being married and living locally and how he was enjoying the hotel. He was flirty, but every time I thought he was becoming too familiar he backed off. Although my pervert antenna kept going off quietly in my head, he always managed to back off enough to make me think I was just being oversensitive.

Then, towards the end of the massage he said he'd been playing sports, had hurt his chest muscles, and could I just massage them for five minutes at the end. Finally, my internal alarm started ringing loud enough for me to pay attention. I said, "I'm not sure if we'll have time."

"Not to worry", he said matter-of-factly, "It's just a bit painful and spoiling my weekend". The alarm turned itself off again. "You just have such an amazing touch." Back on it came. "There's nothing worse than continuous pain is there?" He said. The bell turned off again.

So, I agreed to massage his painful muscles and asked him to turn over. I covered his chest with a towel and asked him to point me to where the pain was. While working on his pecks (the chest), he suddenly and very forcefully grabbed both my hands and put them on his nipples. Then he started moving my hands over them. In hindsight, thank God it was only his nipples!

"Wendy, Wendy!" He said. "You're so beautiful! Come to the hotel tonight, have dinner and share my room with me."

He caught me completely off guard and I just pulled my hands off and said, "Time's up!" Then I rushed out of the room feeling rather flushed.

When he came down to pay, he acted like butter wouldn't melt in his mouth. He winked at me and said, "If you change your mind you know where to find me."

I laughed at his cheek and was more annoyed with myself for not listening to my internal instincts that had been telling me to stop the treatment earlier.

I returned to work the next morning to, unfortunately, find my first client was Mr Cockney.

The appointments were often booked at the spa reception and they always kept the book with them when there was no-one in the salon. The receptionist on this occasion was Danna, a wonderfully larger than life spa manageress who was awfully well spoken and had many years of experience behind her. She had set up the Beauty Department when she was a therapist many years before.

"Danna, I'm not comfortable with this man", I said and told her what had happened the day before.

"Darling", she said. "You poor thing, don't worry, I'll sort it out for you." She then confided that, "He isn't the sort we normally have stay. You know he booked two connecting rooms and bought with him two rather common women, don't you?"

His appointment time of Ten o'clock arrived. Danna suddenly shouted at me, "Darling, darling, quick, hide in the kitchen."

From the kitchen I heard her greet Mr Cockney as lovely as any other guest and send him over to the salon. I laughed at Danna's so-called handling of the situation. It seemed to me that all she did was avoid dealing with it altogether.

"What now?" I said to her. "Don't worry darling, Jean will be in shortly. I'll get her to sort it. Have a biscuit." She said in her awfully posh voice.

Jean, the manageress of the beauty department did sort it. As I did with the young girl and the creepy massage man, she took over the treatment. He was just as flirty with her, but again in these situations, forewarned is forearmed.

When he left the hotel the next day rumours were rife via the housekeeping. They found both rooms in a total mess with empty bottles of vodka and drug paraphernalia scattered about both rooms. Mr Cockney and his two girlfriends had been partying hard, and I was glad to say I hadn't joined in.

As the years have gone on, I've had far less inappropriate incidents while massaging men. Mainly because once I left the spa and went back to high-street salons, there were fewer of them. The ones that did book an appointment tended to be husbands or boyfriends of my ladies.

However, even as an experienced, older therapist I was caught out by one man. He was a gym bunny who came into the salon for a regular massage. His legs were his issue, and indeed he had legs more like steel than muscle. He went to the gym daily and I would give his legs a deep tissue massage twice a week. As the weeks went on, he was complaining about his hips and my massage had to go ever higher up his leg.

I've always enjoyed a challenge and was intent on getting this guy's muscles and joints into working order. So much so, that I just didn't realise to what extent he was enjoying the massage. There were no alarm bells. Firstly, because I was probably old enough to be his mum, and secondly my spa days were long gone, and the radar had gone a little rusty.

My internal alarm failed me completely during the final time I treated him. Towards the end of his massage he suddenly declared how good looking I was for my age. A weird comment, I thought as I left him to get dressed. After he left the salon, I went back into the room to tidy up. Picking up the towel from the coach I discovered he had left rather a lot of creamy discharge. YUK!!

I decided not to investigate too thoroughly and just threw the towels in the wash-bin recommending that they be disposed of rather than washed. Ugh!

We never saw the man again and frankly if he had tried to book, we wouldn't have taken the booking.

To any guys reading this book, next time things are getting out of your control, try thinking of Donald Duck. Perhaps ask to use the loo and splash yourself with cold water! And if this is the sort of massage you require then may I suggest you look for that kind of establishment. There are plenty of 'happy ending' salons about and I'm sure you can tell the difference.

VIP… Aren't we all?

Very Important Person (VIP) would often be written next to a booking in the spa by the management. These guests had to leave the hotel believing it was the best place in the world to stay. Basically, it meant *suck up, and don't mess up*!

So, who did the management deem VIPs?

Journalists:

They would normally stay for free in one of the best rooms. Obviously full-board, so they could experience the wonderful food. They would have full use of the hotel's facilities, including horse riding and spa treatments. This was not only top magazine journalists, but also some smaller newspapers. The hotel was popular with the London crowd, and the management wanted to encourage the high-flyers to spend their money with us. A great way to encourage this was to have a great review in a London newspaper.

The stars:

These guests added prestige to the hotel. After all, everybody likes to stay in a hotel where they may run into someone famous. Don't get me wrong, it was never advertised before their visit.

"FAMOUS AMERICAN COMEDIAN WILL BE STAYING HERE THIS WEEKEND. BOOK YOUR ROOMS NOW."

In fact, it was the opposite, always hush-hush. Often, the booking name would be under an alias, or just an initial. We would first hear about who would be coming during the morning meeting, attended by all department heads. We would also be told about any extra attention they would require.

In our department, this usually meant whether they were grand enough to warrant the Head of Department or most experienced therapist to perform their treatment. We would have to keep the name of the client quiet – even from our staff, until they arrived.

Management didn't want it to get out that some popular singer was staying and risk having a rush of teenagers descending on the hotel. We always kept it top secret.

The extraordinarily rich:

Super rich people came to stay regularly. This could be anybody from super-affluent businessmen who would come down from London for weekends; to the Saudi princess and her entourage who stayed for a week or two every year. The guests who stayed several times a year and so spent a lot of money with us, soon became VIP's in their own right.

The *We-Messed-Up* Guests:

Guests who had had their booking messed up or a returning guest who had left poor comments about one or more departments during their last visit. Obviously, you had to make it up to them and prevent anything from going wrong again. So, we had to go way over the top for them. If it was your department that was flagged, then there was some real sucking-up to be done.

The Owners:

You wouldn't want to upset them because you wanted to keep your job. Management on all levels went into a complete frenzy to make sure everything was perfect for their visit. We literally were at their beck and call. The MD didn't want any negative feedback from them. Though they always managed to complain about something, no matter how hard everyone tried. Once they made a huge fuss just because they found a hair on the floor.

Having said all of that, and despite it sounding a bit of a cliché, all our clients in the Beauty Department were VIPs. We treated each one of them like we would want to be treated ourselves. We prided ourselves on being us, whether they were famous, rich, super rich or a normal everyday working person just treating themselves. The Beauty Manageress made sure that no one person was treated better than any other.

This is what makes a good therapist; treating all your clients like they are VIPs. going above and beyond, making them feel special and ensuring they have a wonderful treatment.

You often had to stay late for the important guests. Not so much for the mess-ups, or the rich, but definitely for anybody famous, royals or the owners. I would often be the one who was called in for a late appointment. I didn't mind, I lived the closest to the hotel and was soon Assistant Manageress anyway. My boss and I also worked well together and always had a laugh. So, I was usually her first call if she needed an extra pair of hands.

On one occasion, I received a phone call on a Sunday evening while we were with some neighbours having drinks. It was the Beauty Manageress asking me if I could come in for a famous sports couple who were arriving via helicopter. They wanted treatments straight away, she told me. She also told me who they were, but not being a sports fan, I was none the wiser.

I explained and apologised to my friends, asking them, as they were big sports fans, if they knew who the couple were. It turned out that the chap played for The Wasps and they were coming straight from an earlier rugby match.

My friends knew the famous couple and got so excited. "Get his autograph! Let us come over as well, we won't get in the way." They said enthusiastically.

Of course, autographs were a big no-no, and I certainly couldn't turn up with my neighbours in tow. So off I went leaving them at home, while all I could think of was how I had to give up my Sunday evening.

My manageress carried out a full-body massage on the lady, and I did the man. He had a rejuvenating facial and I had to be careful because his ear had just been stitched back on from the game he had played earlier. They were both grateful and the man asked me not to tell anyone he'd had a facial. He didn't want to spoil his tough image. They were a nice couple who went on to get married.

That's what being a VIP is all about. We opened the salon especially for this couple on a Sunday evening for two treatments. If this ever happens to you, you know you have made it into the VIP league.

Another time some Middle Eastern royals and their entourage were staying with us for their yearly holiday. They were all female, apart from the bodyguards, who were dressed in black suits. The ladies were also dressed in black, but slightly different as they were in full burkas.

These ladies got lots of preferential treatment. Not only were they spending a huge amount of money, but they were also royalty. Because of their culture, all their meals were taken in the rooms. They were not permitted to be in the presence of other men. Outside of their rooms they were accompanied by bodyguards everywhere they went, who followed them around like sheep.

Waiting on them hand, foot, and finger, hotel management met every need, including late night beauty appointments. They were rather nocturnal and wanted body treatments and facials at 10 o'clock in the evening. They stayed up half the night partying, then slept in until the afternoon. Breakfast was more like lunch, lunch more like dinner.

These ladies never had a conversation with us apart from talking about the treatments or the products they wanted to purchase. They were almost like elegant, black ghosts, gliding in, saying little and just gliding back out again.

I do remember their beautiful made-up eyes, and their amazingly beautiful and expensive underwear tucked away beneath their burkas. You almost felt privileged to be allowed to witness the beauty that lurked beneath, like a secret your average person wasn't permitted to see.

They spent a fortune during their stay. Although we were never paid any extra for coming in for the late appointments, I bet they were charged massively for them by the hotel.

Your average Joe couldn't have treatments after hours. In fact, many guests were disappointed because if they hadn't booked their appointment prior to their stay they couldn't get one on arrival. But if you are royal and spending hundreds of thousands of pounds, just ask and it will be done.

VIP or not, most of the time, guests would get what they wanted when they wanted it. The management wouldn't open the spa after hours for Mr and Mrs Normal, but they were still treated to the highest standard, nevertheless. As I mentioned previously, we are there to serve the guests and do it with pride.

Standards had to be maintained, so certain rules had to be followed, for example, dress code. This meant jacket and tie in the restaurant for the evening meal, and definitely no jeans. On a few occasions some very well-known celebs argued the point, but they always lost. It didn't matter who you were, you were expected to dress well for dinner. Most gave in and borrowed one of the loan jackets and ties – but not all.

A certain very tall comedian was spotted at the local pub with his well-known red-headed, girlfriend. Their evening meal on both nights of their stay at the hotel was taken there. He wasn't going to wear a jacket and tie for anyone, so management didn't let him eat in the hotel restaurant.

As I mentioned before, we welcomed everybody equally. Often this meant putting nervous people at ease and ensuring they could fully relax. Sadly, not all places are like this and I've been to spas and salons where I've been made to feel most uncomfortable. I also know of many therapists that are only nice to the wealthy clients. I hate that kind of arrogance and would certainly not tolerate this attitude from any therapist who worked for me.

A couple from Wales became VIP guests due to their regular visits and spending huge amounts of money.

On their initial visits they were just two working class people enjoying a treat.

They hadn't planned on becoming regulars, but they fell in love with the place. Because of their manically busy working life, they had plenty of money to treat themselves when they had some down time.

Mrs Wales told me she felt like the hotel was her country home, and it was all thanks to the staff that made her feel so welcome. I remember Dana (remember, the awfully posh manageress) getting on well with them.

She would welcome them calling them, "Darlings", just as she would other guests. But I always got the impression she was particularly fond of this couple. I caught her looking at some property deals with Mr Wales (who apparently was a bit of an Arthur Daley), I don't know if that ever came to anything though.

They never had VIP stamped across their booking, but they were always mentioned at the morning meeting as returning guests.

On one repeat visit Mrs Wales turned up for a Sunday morning appointment asking me if I had heard what had happened in the dining room the night before. Of course, I had; rumours circulate fast in a hotel. I played dumb as I didn't want to embarrass her. And she was the type of person who would have hated to think people were gossiping.

She started to tell me anyway. She and her husband had been seated for their evening meal in the restaurant. This was a Michelin Star restaurant, renowned for the food and service. Everything was utterly luxurious, including the beautiful tables and decor. It was as if you were sitting in your very own country mansion. Think *Downton Abby* with small circular tables.

Her husband, who had eaten there many times, was fed-up of the rich food, so he decided he wanted chips with his steak. As he put it, he didn't want more of those, "fancy potato dishes with sauce on." He just wanted chips. So, he asked the waiter, who said he would talk to the chef. The world class chef who, like many of his ilk, tends to think of himself as a cut above us mere mortals, was mortified at this request. "No! This is a world class restaurant, not a cafe." He bellowed at the waiter.

Now, Mrs Wales, who was not one to make a fuss, would have accepted this.

But her husband thought he had spent enough money for his needs to be met. If he wanted chips, then he should get chips. This, he thought was not much to ask for. So, he sent a message back to the chef telling him as much.

Once again, the chef refused, stating in no uncertain terms that if he wanted chips he should go to the local fish and chip shop. Much to his wife's embarrassment, as the other guests were becoming intrigued, Mr Wales asked to see the General Manager. The GM was a lady who ran the hotel with an iron rod. Standards were kept high, but money in the bank was also important.

"I'm sure the chef can manage to make you some chips as you're such a valued guest." She said, when she came to their table.

The following conversation between the chef and the GM was simple. If the guest wanted chips, the guest would get chips. Otherwise the hotel would be looking for another first-class chef.

Later, in the salon with me, she finished explaining the story. Her husband had got his chips but, she said, "The chef still made them as fancy as he could by leaving the skin on and making a homemade tomato sauce which was nowhere near as good as Heinz."

Mr Wales had recognised their VIP status and had begun behaving accordingly. He had realised they could have whatever they wanted. Good for them!

The owners were always VIP's and, of course, the most critical of all the guests. They were a wealthy Greek family and the father and son would often stay for the weekend. The son had a wife and a large family of children and they would come over from Greece with him just once a year to enjoy the luxury. But it was mainly the men who enjoyed the opulence of the hotel several times a year– always with two or three rather gorgeous women.

They would have the best suites in the hotel, with adjoining rooms for their female 'friends'. There was always the same very tall, elegant brunette who seemed to oversee the other girls. The ladies would arrive at the beginning of the weekend to find they had massages booked. Then they would ponder their luxury purchase from the beauty department, which always included a selection of aromatherapy massage oils.

Everything was booked to the owner's account. These ladies were always discreet, and they never told us anything about themselves or spoke about who they were. Were they family friends, girlfriends, or escorts? I'll leave it up to you to decide.

Some people knew they were VIPs and milked it in every possible way they could. The journalists were the Chief Milkers, and who could blame them? They were just ordinary, everyday people, enjoying a few days of luxury. In return they would write an article telling everyone what a wonderful hotel we had.

Journalists were flagged, and each department knew they had to bend over backwards for them. They would always have an hour of pampering booked with Jean, the Beauty Manageress. The most down to earth person you could meet, she made sure they knew that every one of our clients was a VIP to us, and all our therapists and treatments were amazing. We had some great write-ups without ever needing to suck up.

I've massaged and pampered musicians, English and American comedians, game show hosts, actors from films and various soaps, and have even treated a family who owns one of the largest supermarkets in the UK. Some would travel to us in their own cars, some chauffeur driven and a few even arrived in their own helicopters.

Often, I didn't know who the so-called celebrities were. Especially the soap stars. I just didn't watch them; and someone would tell me, "it's so and so from Corrie", and I would just draw a complete blank. Other times, the stars would use an alias or their married name that they didn't use for the screen.

This happened once when a morning television presenter turned-up under her married name. She was a lovely blonde lady, and I had to stop myself from saying, "Oh, it's you!"

One of the American comediennes who stayed with us wanted her nails manicured in her room. In fact, she hardly came out the room the whole time she was with us. We sent one of the young therapists up to do the treatment. This was her first time treating somebody famous and she was really nervous.

We had to calm her down before she went up to the room because she was so star struck. It all went well though and when she came back, she was full of how funny the comedienne was and how she had enjoyed doing the treatment. She also mentioned how tight the comedienne's skin looked, and we had to explain this lady was also famous for her umpteen face lifts.

The majority of the rich and famous were nice people, although they were not always what you expected. The well-known comedian I mentioned previously (the tall chap who didn't want to wear a dinner jacket) and his girlfriend had treatments booked with us one afternoon. This was my daughter's favourite star and I knew it would make her day meeting him. This was the only time I ever broke the rules, and I phoned my daughter telling her to get to the hotel pronto.

In no time at all she was sat in reception hoping to meet him. Unfortunately, he was so far removed from his television persona he was hardly recognisable, being quiet and introverted in real life. He hardly spoke to anyone. My young daughter was really disappointed. Though I will say she fell in love with his other half, who was lovely and chatted to her.

The old saying, *never meet your hero*, springs to mind. In all the years I worked at the spa I never did meet anyone who I could say was a hero of mine. However, many years later I got the chance to massage one of my all-time rock heroes.

He was playing a gig in Bath and one of my clients from my salon knew I really liked him. I had been fed up because I had not managed to get tickets to see him. She was working at the venue and called me saying he had asked for a massage. Could I do it?

Like a bat out of hell, I said yes! Thanks to my lovely client, within a couple of hours, I was stood outside his trailer feeling like a nervous schoolgirl. One of his entourage took me into this amazing trailer, which was almost as big as my house and had every luxury you could imagine. I set up my portable massage chair and they asked how I wanted to be paid. Of course, I asked for tickets to that night's concert, which they were happy to give me.

Then suddenly, my hero was stripping off his shirt right in front of me ready for his massage. I was star struck, just like the young therapist I mentioned just now at the spa hotel. I told myself to stay cool and just do a great treatment. Which I did, being the professional I am.

However, his diva-like attitude and behaviour spoilt the whole experience for me. He hardly said a word to me and made me feel like a servant. After the massage he didn't even say thank you, and just left the room. I was left thinking he hadn't enjoyed the treatment and was much deflated. I packed my chair away and left feeling hugely disappointed.

About an hour after returning to my salon I got a phone call from his PA asking me if I could travel to Southampton the following day to massage him again. But that was my daughter's birthday and we had arranged a small party at home. Explaining this to the PA, I politely said no. Half an hour later she called back. What could they offer for me to reconsider? "You name it!" She said.

He obviously had liked the massage after all. I decided that even if it hadn't been my daughter's birthday, and he had offered me all the tea in China, I didn't want to massage him again.

I went to the concert and enjoyed front row seats, but even that didn't make up for the rudeness of this rock star and my disappointment at meeting him. All those years of hero worshiping blown away in an instant. Sometimes heroes are best kept at a distance.

Home and away

My home salon, or beauty room, came about when I was putting word out to some local salons for some part-time work. I was told a lady who lived in my village was leaving the area and had a small home beauty room. She was looking to pass her clientele on to someone. It was all rather serendipitous.

I met up with her in her lovely home salon – which was very impressive. She had started to run her clientele down since having her two gorgeous twin babies so didn't want any payment for the business. All she wanted was to know her remaining clients were left in good hands.

I spent a couple of weeks working for her while she was getting ready to move home and I was preparing to take on the business.

Excitedly I started to get my little beauty room ready at home. I kept it simple and planned to carry out only maintenance treatments. These are treatments that are required regularly to keep up appearances, so to speak.

Waxing and eye treatments were often considered a salon's bread and butter money. Clients have these treatments regularly throughout the year, where some other treatments tend to go in fits and starts. For example, a client would have regular nail treatments, but only if times were good. If harder times hit, the nail treatments would be the first thing to go. But they would never cancel their waxing, thinking it essential.

I started my home salon in the smallest bedroom, and it was a tight squeeze. But it worked. I had a treatment couch that turned into an upright chair for pedicures. There were a couple of trolleys for equipment and products, and a small table with two chairs which pulled out for nail treatments.

Decorated in a beautiful mint-green colour, it looked both fresh and professional. I named the business, Home Treats. I worked school hours, evenings and some weekends and it was a nice little business. All the clients from the lady's old salon came to me so I had a small clientele immediately. With the help of some advertising in the local parish magazines and word of mouth I gained lots of new clients in no time at all.

I had some lovely ladies, whom I adored. The trouble with this was I enjoyed their company a little too much. I spent far too long with them; either giving them extras for free, or just chatting too much. I was fortunate because working from home I didn't have overheads. Time is money and later when I had my own high street salon, keeping to time was essential for paying the bills. But in my lovely home salon, it was always relaxed and easy going.

I would happily spend all day with some ladies, whereas with others, the full treatment time was plenty long enough. One lady was very particular about her looks, which was obviously good for business. But she always wanted something for nothing and expected me to do more, just because I worked from home.

Now, as I said, I was over generous with my time and my loyal clients always got extras. This lady received her fair share of these perks but was never satisfied. She would really get on my nerves. The whole appointment time would be taken up with her trying to get extras for free. My prices reflected the fact that I was working from home, so she already had a good deal. She also considered the beauty room never closed. She thought because I lived above the office, so to speak, so I should always be available.

"Can't you just fit me in now, after all you are at home." She would plead on the phone. Or it would be, "Could you do a quick back massage after my nails?"

I would explain I had to pick up my children from school so didn't have time. She always had an answer, suggesting she could just hang around while I went to pick up my children, then when I returned, I could do the extra treatment. I had to be firm with this woman, even though extra treatment meant extra money. If I gave in to her once, she would demand more and more.

One time she turned up on my doorstep at ten o'clock at night, exclaiming she had had a disaster. One of her regularly manicured nails had broken and, "Could we just pop upstairs to the salon and put a false one on?" "No, certainly not!" was the definite answer to that one.

You would be amazed, at how single-minded some people could be; in fact, they could be very selfish. A prime example was when my beloved mother-in-law, Renate, died. She had been terribly ill with cancer for a long time, but obviously one never knows when someone will die. We lost her on the Saturday of an August bank holiday. My husband and three children were obviously devastated, as was I. It was difficult for me as it wasn't just losing her, but also seeing my family in such pain.

I had an appointment in the diary for the bank holiday. A lady was booked for a set of nail extensions. I didn't normally work on bank holidays but had said yes as a favour to her. I called her on the Sunday morning and explained that I had just lost my mother-in-law and was so sorry to let her down but needed to re-arrange her appointment.

She wasn't happy. "I realise this was unforeseen, but I don't see why you can't carry out my treatment. It's in your home and it's a bank holiday." She went on to say, "You won't be able to make arrangements concerning the funeral as nobody will be open. For the same reason,

I won't be able to get another salon to do my nails as they'll all be closed."

I tried to explain that the children were upset, and we needed to all be together as a family. But she went on to say, "I want my nails done and you have a responsibility. If you were professional, as you declare in your literature, you wouldn't let me down".

Of course, she did have a point, generally I didn't let people down and, yes, my reputation was important. I tried again to rearrange her appointment for as early as she needed on the Tuesday, but she was having none of it. So, reluctantly I carried out her treatment. I had two very unhappy girls because mummy had gone to work.

When I look back now, I think I should have told her to stuff it. In the grand scheme of things, her nails were not that important. To top it all off, she had insisted on the bank Holiday because she was leaving the village early the following morning. Then I saw her on the Tuesday lunch time going into the local pub.

This woman never came to me again. Good job too! I would never have accepted her if she had.

There were always advantages and disadvantages of having a home salon. One of my problems was that I only lived in a three-bedroom house. This meant my beauty room was small, and all three children were in one bedroom. On the plus side, I was able to work when I wanted and could even work with the children downstairs. It was a good way to earn some money without paying out for childcare.

Eventually, the time came when I needed to separate the children. My eldest daughter needed some space from her little brother and sister otherwise she would have killed them. I was also bored of only carrying out maintenance treatments and my clients were asking for facials and products. With these two things in mind we had a big rearrangement of our home.

We split the large room downstairs in half with a partition wall and had one side as the sitting room/dining area and the other half was mine and my husband's bedroom. My eldest daughter moved into the small room by herself. The other two had the large bedroom and I moved my salon into the middle-sized room.

My new room was wonderful. It had a comfortable chair for pedicures, a table and chairs set up permanently for nail treatments and plenty of room to carry out both facials and body treatments. I also had space to display all my retail products. This was when I invested in my first serious skin-care line, Dermalogica.

Buying into a product line requires a large outlay. You need to purchase all the professional products required for treatments, plus all the retail ones to sell onto clients. I chose Dermalogica because it was one of the first product lines that took skin health seriously.

At the time most cosmetic companies were only interested in instant results, instead of the health of the largest organ of our body. This meant they often used ingredients which, used long term, could cause skin problems.

I knew from experience how debilitating a skin issue could be, and I wanted to treat those unpleasant skin conditions.

My mum suffered with rosacea, a chronic, incurable skin disorder. It can be very debilitating to any person living with it. Back in the seventies there was little help for people with this skin condition. The treatments available were extremely aggressive, causing other nasty side effects. My mum used to suffer, not only with her bad skin, but also with the side effects of the medication. Every time she had a flare-up her self-esteem would plummet. This was where my passion for skin health originally came from.

Until you suffer, or see people suffering, with skin problems you can't understand how really debilitating they can be. I've known people who wouldn't answer the front door unless they caked their face with make-up to cover the problem. I even knew some ladies that wouldn't go out of the house if they had a flare-up on their face.

Over the past thirty years, there have been many scientific advances in skin care. This has led to vast improvements in beauty products. People suffering from skin disorders are, at last, getting the help they need. Thank goodness!

When I first signed up to Dermalogica they were unique, as they had a training institute which provided advance training for qualified therapists. This was one of the first post-graduate training centres. Here therapists were taught about ingredients, good and bad, as well as advanced skin care.

We studied the skin's functions, skin conditions, diseases, premature aging and how to help the client with all kinds of issues. It was one of the best decisions I've ever made in my career, and I've since learnt a great deal from other amazing skin-care companies as well as some doctor brands.

To this day, I am constantly updating my knowledge of how the skin works and what ingredients we can use that will affect its health and look. Dermalogica helped me build my knowledge and passion for skin care, and to this day I specialise in the subject.

Dermalogica did fantastic body products and treatments. Body wraps are wonderful and can be used for all sorts of purposes. There are products that can detoxify, firm, or even help with weight loss.

The weight loss wraps, which enable you to lose inches, are a bit of a weird experience. You are physically wrapped up tight in cling film and bandages. The product tingles and chills until you shiver. You lose inches, so it's a great quick fix for a special night out, but never the most relaxing treatment.

Mud wraps are much more relaxing, and your skin feels soft and smooth afterwards. Unlike the inch-loss wraps, you keep your body warm enabling the skin to absorb the active ingredients. Dermalogica has an advanced mud wrap which produces some stunning results.

When I performed the mud wraps on my clients they would lay on a plastic sheet on the couch. I would boost the circulation by brushing the whole body with a stiff brush. This was followed with a salt scrub, infused with a blend of essential oils exfoliating the skin. After that it was time to apply the green mud, which was thinly painted onto the skin with a large paint brush.

The client was then wrapped in the plastic sheet, a foil space blanket, towels and, finally, a fleece. While they were *left to cook* for twenty minutes, I would treat them to a relaxing scalp massage.

After twenty minutes, I would remove all the blankets from the client, leaving just the polythene sheet wrapped around them. Then I would help them off the couch and into the shower. They would put on a fluffy robe and return to the room ready for a body massage using hydrating oils.

Obviously, I had access to all the products, and I took full advantage of them. So, one afternoon, with no clients booked in, I decided to give myself a body wrap.

The body brushing and scrub was easy and was something I did regularly anyway. The next step: applying the mud and keeping warm while it infused into my skin, wasn't going to be quite so simple. The best option was to apply the mud to as much of my body as I could manage, and then wrap myself in the polythene. Once in the polythene I would go to the heated bathroom, where I would pop a large blanket around me and sit by the radiator. A good plan...or so I thought.

Has anyone ever tried to spread mud evenly over their own body? Probably not, and I wouldn't recommend it.

I began to paint on the mud. I couldn't get to grips with using the brush though, so I soon switched to spreading it with my hands.

By the time I had finished covering myself, I had also somehow managed to flick green mud all over my walls, floor, and beauty couch. It was a hilarious sight, and the whole thing should have been filmed for YouTube.

By the time I had finished wrapping the polythene around myself, I had got mud on both sides of the sheet too. This made getting out of the treatment room, negotiating the hallway, and getting through the bathroom door unbelievably messy. I managed to leave a trail of green mud through the entire house that looked like a scene from a horror film.

By now I was in such a state I didn't even try to wrap the blanket around me.

Instead I just huddled up next to the radiator. And there I was, naked, covered with messy green mud, wrapped in plastic, sitting on my bathroom floor, desperately trying to keep warm. I must have looked a proper state.

I had thought that it would all be worth the hassle for the lovely soft skin I would have after my twenty minutes of infusion. But five minutes after plonking myself on the bathroom floor, the phone started ringing. No problem, the answer machine will get it, I thought. I just stuck my head outside the bathroom door to hear the message.

"Hello Mrs Feltham, this is the school. Your daughter, Georgina, is unwell and she needs to be picked up as soon as possible. As we haven't been able get hold of you, we'll contact your husband instead." Oh no! I couldn't let them call my husband at work; he would be fuming!

I was only five minutes down the road, and he was an hour away. So, in a panic to get to the phone before she hung up, I dropped the polythene and rushed down the stairs still naked and covered in mud. What a sight!

I just managed to grab the phone in time and told them I would be right there. A quick shower to get off the worst of the mud and within ten minutes I was picking up my daughter from school... albeit with green bits of mud still stuck to parts of my body and in my hair.

On our return home, we found the green sludge splashed all over the treatment room, bathroom, hallway, and stairs. To top it off, the infusion had no time to work, so all the effort had been for nothing anyway. Even after the clean-up I was finding bits of green mud stuck to various places in the house for weeks afterwards. Some treatments you just can't do on yourself.

As well as working from home, I've also been a mobile therapist on several occasions. This means that I travel to people's houses to perform treatments. This has been useful when I've been between salons, or when I've needed to be flexible for the family. To this day, I always have a folding couch ready for whenever I need it.

There were some downfalls with being mobile. Firstly, everyone expected the treatments to be a lot cheaper in their home than in a salon. They never considered the time and expense of travelling and setting up. From my point of view, it was worth travelling and setting up if I had a couple of hours of work to do, but not so good if it was only going to be a short treatment.

The secret was not to set your prices too low for individual treatments and offer discounts if they had several treatments at the same time.

Mobile was hard work, lugging heavy beds and equipment in and out of the car and often up flights of stairs. It was always a necessity rather than a choice when I reverted to mobile treatments, and never my favourite type of work. I know some therapists that love it, but not me.

There were additional things you had to be careful about when being mobile. One was not to spill any products in people's homes. I used to take a big sheet to place under my working area. I can be a bit clumsy at times. *My husband laughed at this. He's called me, "A klutz!" on many an occasion.* This sheet has saved me from some expensive wax spills several times.

The other issue was safety. You often worked in the evenings, treating people you didn't know. Both my husband's (I've had two, but not at the same time), were unhappy about me treating men I didn't know. For obvious reasons, I decided to only treat husbands or partners of ladies whom I knew well. This was thought of, by all concerned, as a good compromise.

One therapist, who worked for me in my salon years later, also ran her own mobile business. Unlike myself, she didn't have any concerns about treating men she didn't know. I worried for her and was always telling her to be careful. She was a pretty girl and I felt she was putting herself at risk unnecessarily.

She came into the salon one morning telling a tale of the experience she had with a new client. She arrived at a large house in the countryside and was greeted by an older, extremely ostentatious chap. He was very flamboyant in dress and manner.

The first thing he said when she arrived was, "Wow! You have enormous titties." Although she was shocked, she wasn't concerned because she assumed, he was gay. He was a lot older than her, so if anything, untoward happened she decided she could run faster than he could anyway.

As she was massaging his back, he told her she shouldn't bother getting a boyfriend, but just get a Sugar Daddy. Telling her she wouldn't have a problem, "Bagging one with your enormous boobs." He went on to fill her in on his life story; telling her about his career on the stage and all the men in his life.

She quite enjoyed giving this strange old man his treatment. But when it came time to pay, he had no money on him. He told her, "Just wait here." She thought he was going to pop upstairs to grab some cash, but instead, he disappeared from the house. She was left pacing around for twenty minutes wondering what was going on. He finally returned with her money. It turned out that he had driven to his local ATM to get it.

While she waited alone in this great big house, she found herself reflecting on how unsafe it was for her to be going to homes of men she didn't know. This guy was harmless, but it could so easily have been a different story. After this she changed her rules and only treated men that came recommended, or whom she knew.

Being a mobile therapist, you needed to be extremely organised. Forgetting anything would make you appear unprofessional. If you were unable to carry out the treatment this would be a waste of both yours and your client's time. To ensure I was well organised, I had a great big pull-along toolbox filled with products and tools of the trade. After each working trip I would top up, so would never end up miles from home and missing some vital piece of equipment or product.

I was once listening to one of those radio programs where they confess to things and ask for forgiveness. The story they told was of a new therapist who had turned up to someone's house to perform a back massage. She set up the working area and got the client to lay face down on the couch ready for a wonderful relaxing massage. She suddenly realised she had forgotten the massage oil.

There was no way she was going to risk coming across as unprofessional to this new client. Plus, she didn't want to lose the money. Disguising her panic, she excused herself to wash her hands, and hopefully, find a solution to her problem. The client directed her to the kitchen, and off she went hoping there would be some hand cream in there that would save the day.

There was no such luck, so she checked out the cupboards for some oil, but there wasn't any to be found. Feeling defeated, she suddenly noticed the deep-fat fryer in the corner of the kitchen. She opened it to reveal some relatively clean cooking oil. She grabbed a cup full and returned to the client. To mask the smell, she took her sweet-smelling perfume out of her bag and told the client she was spraying some essential oil around the treatment area.

She proceeded with the massage and the client was none the wiser. After a while, he asked, "Why's the oil a little gritty?" The quick-thinking therapist replied, "I always like to add a little exfoliation to my oils, which is great for getting rid of dead skin cells."

On the radio program, the presenter didn't forgive her! And nor would I have done either. Trust is essential to a good client-therapist relationship. Although I will say there is a part of me that admired her quick-thinking and tenacity.

Friends or clients?

I've never played favourites with my clients, but I did use to look forward to treating some more than others. It just came down to personalities in the end. Some people you just click with more than others, don't you? You simply have more in common or the same sense of humour. Some clients I even considered friends. And others I would like to have been friends with if we had ever had the chance to meet socially.

My philosophies are, *never judge a book by its cover*, and *don't jump to conclusions*. Especially when meeting people for the first time, be it in social or work situations.

People often came into a salon or spa for a first visit appearing rather rude or off-hand. Some, not so professional therapists, would take offence at this and not want to treat them. But I would always see beyond first impressions. Asking myself, what brought them here for this treatment? What was going on in their life to make them appear unhappy or frosty? Were they feeling uncertain about the welcome they would receive and had they had a bad experience in a salon before?

When we feel insecure and a little uncomfortable, we often put barriers up to safeguard ourselves. This can come across as rude, but really, we are just nervous.

When I had my own salon, the rule was that everyone must be made to feel welcome, even if they appeared rude. Nine times out of ten there was a reason behind the way they behaved. Once you got to know them, they were indeed, lovely people, and often became exceptional clients.

One such client, on her first visit to our salon, gave a bad impression to my young therapist, who declared, "She's really snotty and I'm glad you're treating her."

I didn't let this comment change the way I felt about this new client. I was as friendly and professional as I was with all my clients. A quiet treatment progressed and about halfway through she revealed she was in for a treat to cheer herself up. Her brother had recently been found dead, she told me. She wasn't rude, she just wasn't ready to smile and be courteous to everyone at this difficult time in her life.

This lady became a regular client in our salon and would never consider going anywhere else for her treatments. If I had been able to meet with her sociably, I would have liked her to be a friend. She was a very straight-talking lady who said it as it was. But she was also loyal and trustworthy.

She often brought us little presents of plants and home-grown vegetables. I have very fond memories of her, and she is one of many clients I miss. Even the young therapist, who thought she was, "snotty", came to love treating this lady. She eventually became one of her favourite clients too.

In the spa it was not so common to have regulars. We had a few locals who came to us regularly, but being a hotel, we mainly treated one-off guests. However, we had guests who would return frequently and request the same therapist; either because they'd had a great treatment, or just because they liked you.

One client, who I mentioned earlier, came across as being a little off and rude when she first stayed with us at the hotel. But she was just nervous and not used to this kind of environment. All it took was a little reassurance and a smile to put her at ease. She was just a normal working lady who ran a cafe in Wales.

Her hubby dabbled in second-hand cars... and goodness knows what else. I loved it when I saw she was booked in for the weekend. Had the situation been different, I would have enjoyed getting to know her socially.

As therapists, we had to be like chameleons, changing our colours to suit different people. You must learn how to read people and adjust your behaviour accordingly. Part of the job is making them feel comfortable. We must also accept that people are different and what we think of as rude, other people and cultures may not.

I've met, and treated, lots of people from all over the world and some have been more challenging than others. One particular group of Russians spring to mind. They were very demanding and tested everyone to the limit. They were all extremely arrogant. Perhaps this was due to their vast wealth.

They would click their fingers to get our attention or wave their hand to dismiss us. We were addressed as, 'you, girl', which always left us feeling like the servants.

They also seemed to like things in excess. For instance, one of the treatments was a Thalgo Algae Wrap. A 100% natural mud with a high mineral content, which included calcium, magnesium, and a high dose of iodine. With every treatment there are contraindications (medical reasons to not perform the treatment) or contra-actions (reasons that may require you to adjust the treatment).

This wrap was highly active and could affect the hormones and blood pressure of the body. It was recommended to have no more than one treatment per week. Most people had it as a monthly treat. But the Russian ladies wanted one every day for the whole week. They insisted on getting what they wanted, even after we had explained the reasons why this was not ideal.

The Beauty Manageress was at odds with her responsibility as a therapist and the pressure she was under to give the clients what they demanded. In the end, after much discussion, a compromise was reached. They had no health concerns, so it was agreed they could have two treatments in total but not one a day.

Russian ladies are also used to having manicures a certain way. This includes having all the cuticle area cut away, so no cuticle is left. The cuticle is the skin that lies at the base of the nail plate and protects the finger from infection. Now, in a normal manicure you push the dead skin cells off the nail plate and cut away any hanging or excess dead cuticle skin, leaving the living cuticle intact. A lot of Russians want the entire cuticle cut away.

One Russian lady insisted she wanted me to cut all her cuticles away. I refused point-blankly, obviously explaining she could get an infection. At which point, she snatched the cuticle clippers out of my hand, told me I was a "stupid girl", and while I sat there with my jaw dropping to the floor, proceeded to cut away all the skin from around her fingernails until they bled.

Another time, one of them wanted her toenails cut a certain way during a pedicure. We explained to her that this was the reason she had two extremely painful in-growing toenails. We suggested she see a podiatrist as we didn't want to carry on with the pedicure. Yet again, we were told that we were, "stupid girls", and that she had always had her nails done this way.

She demanded we do the treatment exactly as she wanted, and we should just stick some cotton wool under the nail so it would lift the in-growing part. There was really no arguing with these ladies. These clients would definitely not make it onto my Facebook Friends Request list.

Putting up with rudeness is part and parcel of the job and, as I said before, often there are underlying factors. However, there are always exceptions to the rule and one particular lady comes to mind.

She originally booked in with me when I had a room in a hairdressing salon. She was a mature lady in her seventies and very well-to-do. She had been born into money in a different era. The problem was she thought we were her servants and treated us as such. She would always demand an appointment immediately. She was always interrupting us during other people's treatment with no apology and complaining constantly about the price of everything.

In a way, I did feel sorry for her as she had no idea of how to interact with people and had obviously lived a very cosseted life. But although I tried a couple of times to overlook her behaviour, she was just too rude to my other clients. In the end, I just couldn't tolerate her anymore and asked her to stop coming to me.

I would love to tell you lots of tales about rude clients. But over the years, I rarely had to deal with discourteous people. In fact, as I mentioned at the beginning, my clients have mostly been a positive part of my life.

Often when they were down, my heart really went out to them and, although I couldn't change their lives, I could give them a positive experience when they were with me.

A middle-aged lady started to come regularly for a simple lip wax. I'll call her J. When I first met her, she was always well-presented and dressed nicely. She was not a lady who wore a great deal of make-up, but she was always well turned out. She was aloof when I first met her, to the point of being a little rude. But because of her regular appointments I soon learnt she was a private person with a lot on her plate.

She was very embarrassed about the small amount of hair on her top lip, and to keep it at bay, would book a treatment every couple of weeks.

Normally a lady would come for a wax every four to six weeks. But she was paranoid about this tiny moustache and didn't want any hair there at all. I would mainly wax it, but sometimes I would have to pluck, as the hair had not been left long enough for it to be waxed. Occasionally she would come in just a week after her previous treatment for me to check if there was any growth.

No matter how much I reassured her that this type of hair growth was normal; she would not be comforted. She was particular to the point of being obsessed.

She was also very aware of the top lip being left red after the treatment and would insist on sitting in the salon, facing the back wall, waiting for the redness to go down before leaving us. Even when she left, she would have her hand covering her mouth until she got home so no one would notice.

Even though this is obsessive and unusual, you need to remember many things can affect a person's self-esteem, and what may seem like nothing to you may be a big deal to someone else.

Some other therapists in the salon were not so understanding about this lady's obsession, or the fact she hung around so long after her treatment. Whereas I just saw it as my job to help her feel better about herself. So, I would make her feel welcome and get her a nice cup of tea and biscuits while she waited. I also investigated different products to make sure the redness was covered up as best as possible before she left the salon.

I can still see this lady in my mind's eye as she was someone who I really wanted to help but never had the skills or ability to do so. Unfortunately, I watched her self-destruct over the next couple of years. I so wanted to make life right for her; wave a magic wand to make her happy, but there was nothing I could do to help her apart from waxing her lip.

When I first met this lady, she had just recently got divorced from what had been a rather old-fashioned marriage. Her role had been to raise the children and be the home maker; while her husband brought home the bacon, so to speak, and I think they were financially well off.

When her husband left, she was initially still in the family home, but within six months she had to leave. For a while she had a good enough relationship with the ex-husband who was supporting her but that broke down. She was proud of her children. I know one boy was at university and, in the beginning, she had contact with him, but that didn't last either.

I don't know what broke up her marriage. I also don't know whether she drank alcohol while she was married, and if so, to what extent. Maybe the booze came because of the break-up? All I know is, I watched alcohol destroy this lady's life before my eyes.

When she first came into the salon, she was sober and then slowly over the first year I would start to smell drink on her. She would, casually mention about having a lunch-time glass of wine.

After a while it was starting to become obvious that it was more than a lunch-time drink. She sometimes came in to make appointments first thing in the morning swaying and slurring, and she would be all happy, confident, and joking with me.

Often, she attended her appointment with her shopping. The bags would make a clinking noise as she placed them on the floor. First, she would make excuses about the noise, but the longer it continued the less she started to hide the fact that there were always multiple bottles of alcohol in her bags.

After the first year or so she started telling me how she was struggling financially. Amongst other things she would tell me how she had lost yet another flat she had been living in. It was always everyone else's fault. Her husband no longer supported her, and her boys wouldn't talk to her. She never went into detail, but it was obvious to anyone on the outside that she had a big alcohol problem. This was probably causing a lot, if not all, of her difficulties.

For the first year she was still dressed nicely, and remained, as always, overly concerned about her facial hair. She came in regularly and I would always tweak an extra area for free if she noticed any other hair on her face. She was always grateful for the tea and biscuits, and for me putting lots of effort into obtaining different products to cover up the redness. So much so that she always left me a £1 tip as a thank you. I would always try and refuse it; especially when I knew her circumstances were becoming more difficult. But she always insisted.

As time went on, she started to become so drunk in the day that she would often make a scene on our local high street, shouting and screaming at people. She had also started hanging around a pub that was, shall we say, where the less desirable locals would hang out. The deterioration of this middle-class housewife in just over a year was unbelievable. I thought she must be at her lowest ebb, but I was wrong… she had nowhere near reached rock bottom yet.

At one point she disappeared for a few months. I hoped she had got herself sorted and maybe moved out of the bed and breakfast, into a council place of her own. But one day I looked out of the salon window and did a double take. Realising the bag lady hunched over walking down the street, was actually J. She was shuffling along in a dirty old black coat, carrying two big bags.

A short time later she was back in the salon booking an appointment for her top lip to be waxed. When she came for the appointment, she explained how she had been sent to another city to stay in a hostel. Unfortunately, this had not turned out well and she had been very lonely, as well as been robbed while she was there. She had decided to come back to Bath and was sofa surfing while waiting for bed and breakfast accommodation. She slept in someone's house at night, and then had to take all her stuff with her and wander the streets during the day.

With all her problems it was bizarre that she still felt embarrassed about the hair on her top lip. I think this was her one piece of dignity she was holding on to.

One evening I shut the salon up at about eight o'clock, and was heading back to my car, when I saw J with a tatty old suitcase and a sleeping bag at the bus stop. She was very drunk and crying. I went to her and asked, "Are you OK, what's happened?"

She told me there was no one willing to put her up anymore, and there were no bed and breakfasts available. I asked her if she had been to the shelters in the city centre and she told me they had no space for her. I told her there must be someone that could help, and I would make some calls to see if I could find somewhere safe for her to sleep.

Returning to the salon, I took out the yellow pages and called the council, homeless charities, and shelters. I couldn't find anybody who was able to help, and there was nowhere for her to stay that night.

Finally, crying, I rang my husband and told him about the situation. Out of options, I suggested to him I bring her home. He said, and rightly so, that we had three children in the home, and it was our job to keep them safe. He felt it was not

153

advisable to bring a drunk, homeless person into the house.

He also asked what I would do the next morning if I brought her home. Throw her out the next day or leave her in our home on her own?

So, with no real choice, I went back to J to tell her that I couldn't find a bed for her that night and after sitting with her for an hour or so, listening to her drunken ranting, I left her at the bus stop.

Looking back, I remember feeling like the worst person in the world. To this day, I still question my decision to leave her. I wish I had had the courage to take her home with me. If the children had not been there, it may have been a different story.

What happened to J after that? Well nothing much changed. For a while she still came in to see me, albeit less often. I would always book out extra time just to listen to her problems.

She got places to stay now and again, but things always fell through. Eventually, whenever she came in, she would have her blankets in tow and tell me how she now lived on the streets. She was often seen in town with other alcoholics, drinking bottles of cider and sleeping rough.

On a few occasions, she turned up telling me how she had been beaten-up and robbed the night before. Showing me the cuts and bruises she had on her dirty, unwashed body.

No longer was she the well-presented lady I had originally known. Now, all I saw was a homeless alcoholic, with holes in her shoes, who wore her whole wardrobe on her back, carrying her bed wherever she went.

Still, once every six weeks or so she came to me to have her top lip waxed. All I could do was listen to her woes, give her tea and biscuits, and argue with her about not wanting the 50p tip she still insisted on giving me.

At the same time as J was coming to me, I had another client who also had to deal with the unfairness of life. She was a bubbly lady who always came into the salon with a big smile. As usual, as I waxed her, I got to know about her life. She was a single mum of three and had two disabled children. She worked part-time as well as looking after her children; one of whom required round-the-clock care.

I admired this feisty lady who always looked at her cup as being half full and never half empty. She used to tell me how she had to constantly fight to get the best assistance for her disabled children.

One day she came in for, what she called, a quick wax; telling me how she didn't know when she would get the time to come back. She then explained how that afternoon her boy was to be in hospital having his leg below the knee amputated. They had decided that he would be better off with it removed, rather than it being left lifeless just getting in the way.

My heart went out to this lady, as well as my admiration. She dealt with everything life threw at her while still managing to be happy with her lot.

To this day, I wonder where this lady got the strength to, not just cope, but thrive. Why didn't J have that same strength and determination, instead of turning to alcohol for solace?

Why do some people cope, and some don't? I don't know. But I do know that seeing both sides of the spectrum can give you a real kick up the behind.

I still stay in touch with some of my clients. I miss chatting to so many of them over the manicure station. One day, when this book is a success and I'm, hopefully, earning a few more pounds, I'll throw a party for all of them. It will be a gesture of thanks for making my career fun, teaching me gratitude and all the many other life lessons they taught me along the way.

Nailed it

A company called *Back Scratchers* were my first introduction into nail extensions. I first saw them demonstrating at the Brighton Beauty Show and was wowed by the treatment.

I had studied manicures at college, but nail extensions had not been on the syllabus as it was a very new concept in the UK.

These treatments gave your fingernails instant length and were super strong. To achieve this, a plastic tip was glued to the natural nail to give length and then covered with an acrylic substance for strength.

A client would come into the salon with short stubby nails and leave with beautiful shiny long ones. They would return every few weeks to have the growth area filled in. This is known as *in-fills*. At the same time, the nails are filed down and tidied.

Any treatment which meant the client had to return regularly is called a *maintenance treatment*. In other words, it is a great source of regular income for the salon.

When you look at the history of nail extensions, the actual concept has been around a long time. In fact, in the thirties, Greta Garbo had her nails extended with foil and then painted red for filming. The technique took a long time to achieve and then they easily broke, so she always had someone on hand for repairs. Obviously, this wasn't any good for real life, so it never made it into the nail salons of the time.

It was a dentist who created the first acrylic artificial nail in 1934. His name was Maxwell Lappe, and his company Nu Nails is still about to this day.

The acrylic nail really took off in the UK during the eighties. And by the nineties there were hundreds of companies supplying products throughout the country. In the beginning new ideas are expensive, and it takes time for them to become mainstream.

Do you remember how the first DVDs were too expensive for the average household? But soon the price came down and everyone got one. The same is true with new procedures and products.

As the new procedures become popular then more companies offer the products. The increased competition drives the prices down, making it more affordable. This is when the colleges step in and start offering training. Once this happens it's relatively easy, and affordable, for the therapists to get a formal qualification.

Beauty salons and spas, no matter what the cost, must stay up to date and offer the clients the latest treatments to stay competitive. Originally it would be the product companies themselves who trained therapists in these new methods.

Although some of these companies have very stringent rules and require certain beauty qualifications before they train you, others are not so fussy. Companies are, after all, there to make money. And as the competition becomes greater, so often the training becomes weaker. Therefore, a college or beauty school qualification is more sort after as they are guaranteed to maintain certain standards.

However, when the treatment is new beauty salons would send just one person for the initial training. That therapist would then be expected to pass the information on to the rest of the salon's therapists. The problem with this is that knowledge often becomes diluted. Think Chinese whispers!

The nail industry grew extremely fast in the first few years. Smaller companies were quick to jump on this money-making treatment. They started to offer the products to anybody and everybody, and they didn't require you to have any formal beauty qualifications first. Soon, it wasn't just beauty salons that recognised the money-making potential. Hairdressers and individuals were jumping on the bandwagon too.

You no longer needed any certificates to prove you were proficient in the beauty industry and anyone could purchase nail extension products. If the client was lucky, the girl doing her nails may have carried out a one-day course. But they often had no training at all. The phrase, *nail technician* was suddenly being used by anyone who stuck nails on the end of a finger or five.

You can do a lot of damage to someone's nails and this was proven far too often in those early years. Unfortunately, it can also still be true today. Buyers beware! There are people out there (maybe in a salon near you) who really shouldn't be carrying out this type of treatment.

One day, early in my training, I was removing my acrylic extensions. This was done by buffing off the overlay with a nail file. The original acrylics were very thick, so this was a time-consuming job. You had to make sure you were filing the acrylic substance off and not the nail plate.

This is a precise procedure requiring you to have a very harsh-grit file positioned at the right angle to remove the product. While filing the substance off one of my nails I was inadvertently catching part of my natural nail. I suddenly realised I had filed not only the acrylic but the natural nail as well - to the point of exposing the nerves underneath. Ouch!

There is a reason pulling off fingernails is such an effective torture method. Just the air touching these exposed nerves was excruciating. I had learnt a painful lesson right at the beginning of my training which ensured I would never repeat this mistake on anyone else.

In my high street salon, we were always having people turn up, with their nails in a bad way after suffering poor removal of their extensions. In severe cases the nails can be damaged permanently.

This got worse over the years as mechanical nail files were introduced to make removal quicker. The trouble with these types of files was that they could also, cause intense heat, which could burn the nail and surrounding skin. It was too easy to over-file and damage the nail plate, as well as the surrounding skin. Add to this a chatty therapist, not paying attention, and you get some nasty results.

Nowadays, we are also more aware of the chemicals used in the beauty industry. As consumers, we no longer just look at the results regardless of how they are achieved. We want to know about the chemicals we are placing in and on our bodies - and rightly so.

When the nail extensions were first available there was little information about the chemicals that were used and no evidence of the long-term health implications for the therapist or client. For anybody who has not smelled acrylic, it has an extraordinarily strong pungent smell. It is obviously not a natural product, but one that comes from chemicals.

I was fortunate enough to train with one of the leading companies of the day in acrylic and gel products. The non-acrylic gel smelled far less and required no buffing off. Right from the beginning, I felt that acrylics couldn't be good for you. It was obvious from just that awful smell. There had to be consequences.

In fact, sadly, I knew a couple of the trainers in the industry that had been using these acrylic products for years and had, over time, developed lung cancer. Now, there was no evidence to prove this was caused by the nail products, but it was not a chance I was willing to take. So apart from the training, I've never used acrylic products.

The first acrylic formulas developed for nails contained methyl methacrylate, a strong chemical that eventually was found to be hazardous. Nowadays products must not contain this by law. But this is not policed very well and there are unscrupulous or uninformed people that still use these banned products today; mainly because they are cheap.

Acrylics are constantly changing and being refined. Improving not only the look you achieve but also the chemicals applied. Even with the low odour products though, we can't get away from the fact we are dealing with chemicals. A fact which most of us overlook for the sake of beauty.

My first aim when consistently applying extensions to clients is to look after their natural nails. I would always use first class products and opted to use a gel, rather than acrylic. Gel, in my opinion, is better for your natural nail as it tends to be more flexible and thinner.

Many people prefer acrylic because they are strong, and they think their nails won't break as easily. But that strength can be misleading. The acrylic extension may not break, but the natural nail beneath can do so. This can lead to painful bacterial infections under the overlay.

Personally, I like to recommend my clients periodically give their nails a rest from having extensions or overlays. No matter what any nail technician or therapist tells you, there is always a certain amount of deterioration of the natural nail. If it's covered constantly with a product you cannot nourish the nail. Sunlight, oils, and creams are a must for strong healthy fingernails.

Whether you choose a gel or acrylic, a good technician is essential for the health of your natural nails. Knowledge and experienced is vital for the care you deserve.

Here are a couple of things to think about before you have nail extensions, and in fact, any beauty treatment:

Firstly, check the qualifications of the person doing your nails or beauty treatment.

Secondly, and especially important, ask what products are being used. Then check they are a good standard on the internet prior to your appointment.

Thirdly, remember the best advert is word of mouth.

And finally, cheap treatments tend to mean inferior products and unqualified therapists. You get what you pay for!

There are a lot of nail shops that have popped up over the years in every high street. They generally have an oriental influence and I call them *the chop shops*.

Now, I'm not saying all these walk-in nail shops are the same. I am sure some can perform great treatments and their clients are happy. However, during my career I've seen continuously poor practises from these salons. Here are just a few horror stories I've come across.

A lady was having her nails done in such a place when, suddenly several men walked in and started talking to all the staff in a foreign language. Other men were running around checking the rest of the building. The official told her that she had to leave, and her treatment could not be finished, because they were closing the salon.

There was a great deal of shouting and confusion as people from upstairs were escorted out by, what turned out to be, the immigration officials. Later we learnt these were the 'nail technicians' living in one room, above the salon. They were unqualified and worked illegally for a pittance.

I personally feel the client with the half-finished nails had a lucky escape, no matter how inconvenient it was for her. Who wants to benefit from this type of slave labour? Not to mention the possible damage that could have been done to her nails. At best, some of these places use unqualified labour and cheap, sub-standard products; at worst they use banned, carcinogenic substances.

We had a good reputation in our salon, especially for nail treatments. So, of course, we often had people coming for help after having bad experiences elsewhere. They were usually ladies explaining how their nails were burning under the acrylic, and they wanted them removed. We could only help so much by removing some of the substance. We would risk damaging the natural nail more if we tried to file it all off in one go. It was a case of growing out the product with our help and some regular trips to our salon.

To get their nails back to a good condition, it would cost them much more in the long run, than the cheap nail extension they had originally opted for.

One of the worst cases I saw was a lady who came into us asking for help, two months after her disastrous treatment in a chop shop. What was left of her natural nails was in a horrendous state. They were grooved, splitting, and crumbling away. "My nails make my hands look ugly," she told us, "Could you put nail extensions on to cover the mess while they grow?" They were so bad we took pictures and wrote a full account of what had happened to protect ourselves from any come back.

She explained it had been a spur of the moment treat. She had strong, healthy nails but due to the type of work she did, they were kept short. So, as it was Christmas, she decided she would have some beautiful, long, red nails for the occasion.

As she put it, "I wanted to look glam for some Christmas and New Year parties." She had seen the salon in town before and there were always people in and out, so it was obviously popular. The salon worked on a walk in and wait basis, so in she went for her Christmas treat.

She hadn't known what to expect and told us that the procedure had been painful. Never having had nail extensions before she thought, at the time, this was normal. There was little English spoken, so she couldn't really communicate her concerns. After a mere twenty-five minutes she had long, red nails, but she was also left in a lot of pain. She mentioned this to the lady as she paid and in broken English, was told, "Pain will go away."

But it didn't! After a day with a continual burning feeling under her extensions, she couldn't put up with it any longer. She returned to the salon and asked for them to be removed. She was told, "Pain perfectly normal - it will go away later."

Leaving it a further day or two, she finally had enough and returned demanding the extensions be taken off. The removal was agony as they buffed the acrylic off with an electric file. Though the product had gone on like a gel, unbeknown to her it was acrylic. She allowed them to continue removing the coating thinking of the relief she would feel once they were off.

The shock of what she was left with made her burst into tears. Her nails were left red raw, with layers of the nail filed completely away to reveal the nerves below. Her cuticles were left bloody and ripped from the over-zealous filing.

Within days the pain worsened, and pus was oozing from the nail plate and cuticles. She went to the doctors, where she had to have her hands bandaged and was put on a course of antibiotics. This was not at all what she had in mind for the party season.

When we saw pictures of the original damage, even with our awareness of poor treatments, we were left completely speechless. It had taken two months to heal and she was left with short, ugly, hollowed out nails.

We assured her we could help with the look of her nails, though we couldn't guarantee they would ever be strong again. We applied a short extension to cover the mess while her natural nail grew back underneath. We used a top product that was flexible and breathable. She had to return to us every two weeks to check how things were going, and once every four weeks for an in-fill.

We eventually soaked the coating off, and she went on to use treatments that helped to repair the damage left on her natural nail. She would never have strong nails again, but they were reasonably healthy once we finished doing our bit. It took well over a year before she had her own healthy nails back.

The lady tried to make the chop shop accountable through a solicitor. Unfortunately, they had covered their behinds thoroughly. All their so-called nail technicians worked freelance, and this one had moved on. How convenient! That chop shop is still open for business to this day.

This was probably the worst case of damaged nails I've come across, but I had many ex-chop shop clients with even more stories to go with their terribly damaged nails. One of my clients had her nails done; and during the treatment had complained about the young girl who didn't speak English, hurting her. The lady, in charge said, "Please bear with her, she's still learning."

I had reports from other ladies telling me how they had seen 'nail technicians' arriving in their school uniforms before changing and doing treatments. These girls could not possibly hold a professional qualification. And they most certainly would not have been able to obtain any kind of insurance.

There was often no sense of health or hygiene in these places. If you looked close enough you could see they were grubby and dirty. The implements were used from client to client without any sterilisation in between. The risk of cross contamination being a huge issue.

These places also offered pedicures. One would wonder what harm could be done with a mere pedicure. But it's one of the easiest ways of passing on nasty fungus or bacterial infections. The first line of defence from contracting these nasty infections is for the therapist to check each client's feet prior to the treatment.

People were always telling me how no one ever inspected their feet to check for contraindications before a treatment. There was no such thing as infection control in these places, and often no safety procedures either.

The worst safety issue I was told about was from a lady who decided to get up halfway through her pedicure and leave. She had chosen a local chop shop to have a spur of the moment pedicure. She was relaxing, with her feet in an electric foot spa, with the water bubbling away. Then she happened to move her eye from the magazine she was reading, only to notice the bowl was split and water was seeping out onto the electrical plugs right next to her chair. She obviously knew electrics and water didn't mix. She immediately realised the danger and removed her feet from the hazard and left the salon.

I've seen all sorts of poor-looking nail extensions, and they were not all from the chop shops. Some were from salons that should have known better. There were gels and acrylics applied so thick that they looked like brightly coloured horses' hooves. I've seen permanent French polish finishes where the white tip came halfway down the nail, instead of just covering the free edge. This, to me, always looked like porn star nails.

Sometimes the nail tips were applied so wide they overlapped the cuticle edge around the nail. At best, they looked ridiculous, at worse, they would peel straight off. Or there were nail tips which spread out either side of the fingertip like a fan. All the above could transform your beautiful, natural nails into something cartoon-like.

Even today, when the profession is supposedly regulated, there are still so many of these chop shops around. I still hear horrendous stories about people suffering pain and permanent damage because of visiting them.

Before nail extensions became popular, manicures were the main hand treatment available in salons. These took just as long as a full body massage, but you charged less than half the amount of a massage treatment. Even though, you often used expensive products and the preparation time was longer – because of the cleaning and sterilising of utensils after each treatment.

A typical manicure would include exfoliation of the hands, cutting and shaping the nails, removal and tidying the cuticles, hand & arm massage and finally, four coats of colour. To get all of this done you had an hour booked and sometimes a mere forty-five minutes.

If this was a regular client, it was relatively easy to do. However, clients would turn up for a manicure for a wedding or special occasion having never had a manicure before and with their nails in a terrible state. In these situations, an hour seemed no time at all.

Ladies who kept horses, kitchen workers and cleaners had the worst hands of all. They would often have ragged, overgrown cuticles with hangnails. These are the splits in the skin which start at the base of the nail and travel vertically down the skin on the finger, which is very unsightly and painful. Then there were the nail biters. I can't even describe how difficult it is to make these nails look great for a special occasion.

We were so often miracle workers, and it was a huge sense of achievement when you sent someone away with half-decent looking hands and nails.

A one-off manicure could not solve all problems, but it could be the start of someone changing their bad habits and looking after their hands and nails properly. Often people would say, "I don't have any nails so there is no point in having a manicure." This is actually the perfect time to have a manicure. It's a time when a therapist can give you some good advice on how to look after your hands and nails, and help you stop causing further damage.

We had many ex nail biters coming in for help and advice, and the first thing we would recommend was a regular manicure. Over the years, I had many success stories and often someone who had bitten their nails all their life would end up with healthy strong nails after coming to me regularly.

Some nail biters were left with permanent damage such as spoon-shaped nails. This is a common problem after biting your nails for years. Another problem is if you have been a picker or biter of the cuticle for a long period of time. Once you stop, the cuticle has often been over stimulated. This leads to it growing halfway up the fingernail. This again, is a problem that will not change but can be kept under control with regular manicures and homecare.

One client, Maggie, decided to stop biting her nails in her later life. She came to us for a manicure because her cuticles were ragged and halfway up her nails. She came for a regular manicure every four weeks for many years. While I was tidying up her cuticles, I would have a good moan at her if she had picked them, or if she hadn't been wearing gloves for chores. At which point she would look all sheepish and apologise.

We would chat about everything, and she became much more than a client. We got to know each other well, and I was very fond of her. She would do some sewing and alterations for me and we would put each other's worlds to right, over the manicure table. This, for me, is the attraction of a regular manicure treatment. It wasn't just the kick I got from my clients leaving with lovely nails, it was the fact you could chat and make a real bond with people.

I would find out about their lives, and sometimes their rather lavish lifestyles. Mrs M, another regular of mine, when not in her London home, travelling the world, or on her boat, always came to me for her manicure. This lady lived in a different world to me, her husband, through hard work, had enabled her to have a wonderful lifestyle.

She would tell me about a birthday bash she was off to where Sir Elton John was the entertainment. Or how she was off to a shooting weekend, or the girl's getaway she was hosting in the Caribbean. She was always rushing here and there, organising refurbishment of her properties, as well as fitting in quality time with her sons and grandchildren.

Her husband, even though nearing retirement age, took barely any time away from his work. I think her favourite time was probably putting her feet up at their country home, which, apparently, didn't come often enough. I loved hearing about her wonderful lifestyle, but would I have swapped? I don't think so. It was way too hectic for me.

I've always enjoyed nail treatments as they are great for when you feel like a good chat, and of course, they are also far less strenuous than massage and waxing. On the other hand, sometimes you didn't want to be that sociable, so a quiet facial and massage was ideal. That's one reason why I liked my job so much. I could do chatty and social as well as quiet and chilled. After all, variety is the spice of life.

My ideal day would be when a little of everything was booked in. Although by Friday or Saturday afternoon, after a physically strenuous week, I was more than happy to just chat while painting nails. In my high street salon, we often ended the Saturday with a couple of regular nail clients chatting over tea and cake.

Bridal parties were another buzz. The bride, the mum and bridesmaids always brought a great atmosphere with them. If they were spending lots of money, or if they had been our clients for some time, out would come the fizz and chocolates. This was always good fun.

We had one bridal party on a Thursday evening. They were having gel overlays so they could go out with dry nails; ready to travel straight to the venue, which was some miles away. We had finished one set of nails when suddenly the power went out. No electricity meant there was no UV lamp to cure the gel and no lights to see what we were doing.

Even the streetlights were off, and it was a rainy winters evening. We frantically called the electric company to find out what was going on. They informed us that it was a severe problem, as the engineers had cut though power lines. They had no idea when the power would be back on, but it wouldn't be any time soon.

My poor bride and her mum; they were the most important part of the bridal party and the last two still waiting for their gel nails. We were all coming up with different suggestions and possible solutions. They couldn't come back the next day as they were travelling to the venue that night. We tried calling other salons that had power, but they were either booked-up or not open. Maybe we could come to the venue the next day? This wouldn't work either as they had other commitments.

After waiting a short time to see if the lights would come back on, we eventually had to scrap the gel and go for painting the nails with ordinary polish. We pulled the manicure stations as close to the large window as possible to get as much light from outside. This included turning on my car lights.

By torchlight and car headlights our bride and mum finally had their nails manicured and polished ready for their big day.

Some brides are more demanding than others and some are purely and simply Bridezillers. We once had a bridesmaid having nail extensions. She was chatting about the upcoming wedding, telling us how she wasn't particularly looking forward to it.

The bride, apparently, was a complete Brideziller. She was demanding all sorts of things, including colour co-ordination of all guests, and every lady having to wear a hat... otherwise they would not be welcome. But everyone agreed she had crossed the line when she told her own sister that her ears were sticking too far out, and when her hair was up it would ruin the wedding photographs. The bride even offered to pay for her sister's ears to be pinned back surgically.

I couldn't believe what we were being told. I asked the friend, "had the sister ever mentioned to her about having cosmetic surgery on her ears before?" She said this had been the biggest issue. Nobody had ever mentioned the ears sticking out. The poor girl had never even thought there was a problem with her ears.

This obviously caused a great deal of upset and left the sister in tears. They had never been that close, but this completely ruined any relationship they did have. At that point in time, all that was known was the sister had refused the surgery.

I never found out if she still agreed to be a bridesmaid, or if she even went to the wedding. All I know is, no matter how perfect that wedding looked on camera, I'm sure it wouldn't have been a happy occasion. I know I wouldn't want to attend such a false-fronted event myself.

Often nails would be a last-minute thing for brides. I always found this hard to believe, as I've always booked my nails well in advance for any key event I attend. In fact, it's the first thing I notice about people; what their hands and toenails look like. Not so much whether they are long and polished, but whether they are clean, shaped, and well cared for. A big no-no for me is chipped nail colour and dirty nails, especially on someone serving me. If you were getting married why would you not think nails straight away?

Some brides would turn up the day before their wedding, or even the morning of the wedding, demanding something be done to their appalling nails. We always tried to fit them in, but as a busy salon it wasn't always possible. If we couldn't do their nails, I would recommend other salons and warn them against the chop shops.

I loved it when I could sit across from the bride and chat about the up and coming event. I would always ask after the groom, and talk about how they first met, etc. But after I was told a couple of times that it wasn't a groom, but rather another bride they were marrying, I learnt to ask about their partners instead of the groom.

Whether it was same sex or opposite sex marriages, I always suggested their partner come in for a manicure as well. After all, their hands would be in the ring photos too. Some brides did manage to get their man to come in and they presented another challenge all together. The worst were motor mechanics. They always had split, chipped nails and ingrained dirt in their fingertips. Sometimes, we really did perform miracles.

We also got to hear all the gossip. We often learned who had had affairs with whom over the manicure station. Our ladies would share with us what they thought of their children, husbands, and families. They would tell us about the latest diet they were on, as well as their latest medical test results.

In some cases, they even shared intimate details of their cancer treatments and how they felt. Often sharing with us feelings they kept secret from their own families. Sitting across the table from someone doing their nails was another treatment that seemed to loosen tongues.

They would often tell us all kinds of secrets and we would be the listening ear; trying not to take sides or judge. I would often say to the girls who worked for me that they must never repeat anything they hear and must never have too much of an opinion. We were there to listen and not judge, though in the case of some ladies that could be extremely difficult.

Sometimes, you would just want to reach across the workstation and physically shake the client; especially those who were being abused in some way. There was one very glamorous lady in her late twenties who was a criminal's *moll*. She had a sports car and a flat, which were both provided by him. At first glance, she seemed to have an amazing lifestyle. She even had a wonderfully exotic name. But treating her regularly, you got to know there was a heavy price to pay for her trips to Marbella, all her beauty treatments, and her expensive clothes.

She was the eye candy that had to look perfect. She was at this man's beck and call, always to be seen and never heard. She knew, as did everyone else, he had his wife and family who came first. They were the ones with all the security and a home in Bath. The wife stayed at home and the eye candy travelled everywhere with him. When he told her to jump, she would ask how high.

Sometimes she would turn up with bruises and even a broken arm one time, from where he had pushed her down the stairs. She would cry about how badly he treated her and there had been several suicide attempts. This was a time when you just couldn't keep quiet and you had to tell her how wrong this situation was.

We used to tell her how she deserved so much better. She would listen, cry, and agree, but life always stayed the same. He was the love of her life - or perhaps the lifestyle was. Maybe she just didn't know how to get out of this abusive relationship. Who knows? I hope something positive and good became of her in the end.

After years of being in the industry, less and less shocks you, even when people went out of their way to try to embarrass you. There was the lady who walked into the salon and came straight to the manicure station where someone was having a treatment and asked for a quote for nail extensions. Shock value was what she was looking for. After telling her the price for a set of nails, she placed her hands on the table to reveal only three fingers on each hand.

"How much for these?" she said, with a rather cheeky smile on her face.

She wanted a reaction, but my colleague was as cool as a cucumber and just said, "I'm sure we can give you a discount."

In fact, my colleague was great when dealing with clients who wanted to make a scene. Some people expect miracles from their nail extensions, gel overlays or even a nail polish. Of course, they don't last forever, and, of course, sometimes they break… especially if they are treated badly. For instance, if you have a manicure and then return home and put washing-up gloves on, you are going to ruin the nail paint.

People will complain, and sometimes it's your fault and sometimes it's theirs. Sometimes we will fix it free of charge and sometimes we won't let a client get away with trying it on....and why should we? We are running a business. You wouldn't buy a new silk dress, and then go horse riding in it and return it to the shop because it had snags everywhere, would you?

I applied a French polish gel to a lady one Saturday morning. She was off to a school reunion and wanted to look good. She was happy with her finished result, as indeed, was I. In fact, she was so pleased that she bought a voucher for her teenage niece to come and have a mini makeover. We wished her a great time that evening and that was that.

Two weeks later, on a Friday afternoon, she came into the salon. The young girl on reception greeted her as I was attending to two young girls waiting to have their ears pierced. The woman, at the top of her voice, said, "I want to talk to her", pointing at me. I excused myself from the girls and their mothers and went over to the client asking how she was and did she have a good reunion. "No!" she said, "look at the state of these nails." I was shocked by her aggressive attitude as she had been a happy, friendly lady last time I had seen her.

I inspected her nails and explained they had lasted well. But after two weeks the nail grows, and the white tip moves away from the finger, which leaves a gap that looks like you have dirt under the nail. However, I explained that this can be rectified by either in-filling them and repainting the tip or soaking them off.

She was becoming loud and aggressive and telling me I had done a rubbish job with her nails; suddenly declaring, "Everyone at the reunion said my nails looked awful."

Well, I couldn't believe it. Her nails looked lovely when she left the salon. Once again, I explained that after two weeks they needed to be sorted. At this point she went off on one, shouting and swearing about wanting her money back. Her poor husband was behind her and he just stood looking at the floor, obviously mortified. He touched her arm to calm her down, but she pushed him aside as she yelled about my, "shoddy work."

I was really struggling to understand what was going on because it was so unexpected. She had certainly achieved the shock factor with me. This was when my colleague stepped in and came to my rescue. She asked her to calm down as there were children and other clients in the salon. But this request just made her even more angry and aggressive.

"Look at these filthy-looking nails, I'm a businesswoman I can't have them looking like this." She shouted. My colleague looked at her nails and agreed with what I had been telling her. She then told her she couldn't come in and complain about her nails two weeks after having them done. If she had truly been that unhappy, she should have returned immediately, and we could have rectified her concerns at the time.

"I didn't realise how rubbish they were until I was told my nails were awful at the school reunion." She declared ferociously. This didn't sound right to us. Who would really look at someone's nails and declare that they looked rubbish?

"Well you were happy at the time. In fact, you were so happy with the treatment you bought a gift voucher." My colleague reminded her.

To which she replied, "I want my money back for the voucher as well as for the nail treatment, otherwise I'll bad mouth you and give you a bad review online."

By now, everyone in the salon was listening and cringing. I was apologising to the girls' mothers who were waiting for their treatment. I suggested they go into a room to keep the girls out of ear shot of this woman as her language became worse.

Suddenly, my colleague lent over the counter sniffed the air and said, "Have you been drinking madam?"

I can still remember her bright-red face getting angrier as she declared, "I may have had a glass of wine but that's none of your business."

My colleague picked up the phone and said to the husband standing behind this woman, "I will not be giving any refund, as there is nothing wrong with the nails. If there was a problem or you were unhappy with your nails, then you should have come back the same week the treatment was done. Your wife is being abusive, and I'm going to call the police unless you remove her from my premises."

The poor man just nodded, grabbed his wife, and dragged her out of the salon. They stood outside the shop arguing for a moment, and then they walked off in separate directions.

To this day, I cannot understand why this woman had come back to complain. Did she just want her money back? Had she drunk too much alcohol? Did she have a rubbish reunion so decided to blame us? Who knows?

However, there was some karma after this outburst in the salon. About half an hour later, she came back and asked very sheepishly if she had left her car keys behind as she had lost them. We were very polite and looked for the keys everywhere but didn't find them. We couldn't help but feel a little smug as she left empty handed. The whole salon had the attitude of what goes around comes around.

Another fine mess

I've always been extremely cautious and carried out the required patch tests and consultations to ensure the treatments I give are safe. It's important to know what medication people are taking, as this can affect the skin's sensitivity. We also need to know about the health of the person we are treating for lots of different reasons.

I always try to explain it's not that I'm being nosy, but certain conditions affect the way I would carry out a treatment. For example, someone with diabetes can have thinner skin and poor healing capacities, so we wouldn't carry out certain treatments and would vary others accordingly.

Another example is when performing a facial. It helps if you know if someone is under a lot of stress, or what skin care products they use. This can help us treat the problem they have come in for.

Still, some people don't understand the importance of telling us about their health issues, or they just forget to tell us at all.

I was once in the spa performing an electrical galvanic facial. This involved running metal rollers over the face. We had carried out the consultation and nothing came up to contra-indicate the treatment.

I had performed many of these facials and loved doing them as much as my clients loved receiving them. The music was playing, the client was cosseted, and everything was warm and relaxed. I had almost drifted off into hypnosis, which was something that happened often when I was rolling the face. This part of the facial is almost as relaxing for the therapist as it is for the client.

I suddenly heard this rhythmic ticking. I knew it wasn't on the music, or in my head, and suddenly realised it could only be one thing. Oh my God! This lady hadn't told me she had a pacemaker.

You should never perform any electrical treatment on someone with one fitted. I immediately stopped the treatment and asked her if my assumption was true and why she hadn't told me. She said she had had the pacemaker for so long it hadn't crossed her mind to mention it. Yes, it would be highly unlikely for the current to affect the pacemaker, but on the other hand, you really wouldn't want to risk it, would you?

After that, I always asked clients if they had pacemakers, or metal plates they may have forgotten about before I did any electrical treatments. Most people looked at me like I was on another planet, but I wasn't ever going to take a chance of not knowing again.

Another lady failed to tell me she was six months pregnant before I performed a massage on her. It wasn't until she turned over on her back that I noticed the smallest neatest little bump I had ever seen. "You didn't mention your pregnancy", I said.

"No, I'm past the four months, so I didn't think it was necessary." She said. "Most people don't realise I'm six months pregnant as I've got such a small bump."

What she didn't realise was that we were using a pre-blended essential oil product. The one I was using was safe to use in pregnancy. But the one she nearly chose, the Energising oil, contained

Jasmine oil which can bring on contractions.

Again, a lesson learned for me. No matter what the age of my client, I always asked if they are pregnant or breast feeding. For older clients, I would always make light of it saying, "Obviously you're not pregnant or breast feeding?" Adding a wink at the end.

I always erred on the side of caution. You never know people's ages. I made it a rule long ago never to guess how old anyone was if they asked me too. The last time I did that, I guessed the lady was forty and she said indignantly, "I'm only thirty!" This was a double shocker, as I had already knocked a few years off my first guess.

It's a therapist's responsibility to make sure they only carry out the treatment if it's right for the client. Some salon owners, especially those who are not trained therapists, often don't realise it's better to lose the money and gain the trust. You don't want to risk something going wrong and face a ruined reputation and a possible insurance claim.

I always tell the girls I'm training that it's their responsibility to say no to a salon owner if they are being asked to do something, they know is wrong. It's the therapist who will be sued, have a ruined reputation and probably not be able to get insurance in the future. Despite this, some therapists are put under huge pressure to carry out the treatment because the salon doesn't want to risk losing the money.

But no matter how cautious a therapist is, things do go wrong, and what matters most is putting it right afterwards. We must always remember that we are only human, and mistakes happen. A common mistake made by therapists is taking too much off the eyebrow hair when they're shaping them, and the brow ends up too thin for the client.

It often happens, especially with newly qualified therapists, and unfortunately, you can't stick the hair back on with glue. With all new clients, and with the help of a hand mirror, I discuss beforehand exactly what shape is wanted, and I'm always honest about expectations.

I can't make a lady's brows look like Cheryl Cole's if they aren't the right shape in the first place. I would have to explain that we can only work with what we have. After all, you can only ever look like you.

When you do take too much off, and it has happened to me earlier in my career, you can only say how sorry you are and not charge them for the service. As a rule, I try to take less, rather than more. But sometimes you can misunderstand someone and still end up with a dissatisfied client. Unfortunately, it happens.

I'm just as careful with eyebrow tinting. It's so important, especially when treating someone for the first time, that you check the type of hair they have so you can assess how quickly the tint will take. I would also apply and remove tint in the shortest amount of time, so I could get the client to check they were happy with the colour and reapply if they wanted them darker.

Some clients like them dark, which is currently the fashion. Others want hardly any colour at all. Older ladies, especially, don't want their brows tinted too dark. I've had ladies come in the salon feeling devastated and asking if I can remove the colour from their brows as another therapist had overdone it. They would liken them to two dead, black slugs sitting above their eyes. There is never anything I can do and can only assure them it will fade with time and eventually grow out.

I'm always flabbergasted to hear how a therapist can apply the tint on the brows without a proper consultation with the client as to her desired result. They just throw the tint on for a standard time and remove it, leaving dark slugs for everyone.

If a client of mine isn't sure whether her tint is dark enough, I tell them to live with it for a couple of days and come back for a top-up if they want more colour.

The worst thing nowadays is a dark brow which has been inked on. Semi-permanent make-up and eyebrow micro-blading are a great answer for ladies who have hardly any eyebrow hair. This lack of eyebrow hair may occur for several reasons: over plucking when we were younger, chemotherapy, natural hair loss as we get older, or perhaps some people have never had much hair in the first place.

It's like having a tattoo; ink is placed into the skin via tiny needles. The ink doesn't go in as deep as a traditional tattoo, so is classed as semi-permanent rather than permanent. After about two years you are left with a faded colour, so you need to have the ink topped up to keep it at its best.

This treatment can make a huge difference to someone's face. Giving the eyes definition in this way can make someone look ten years younger and increase their confidence massively.

Talking to the client prior to this treatment is essential. A good therapist would discuss the procedure and outcome before sending the lady away to think about it before she agrees to go ahead. Your face can look quite different if you have never had much of a brow and then suddenly you do.

In the right hands this can be a great treatment. Unfortunately, as I mentioned previously, not all manufacturers provide good training. And as this money-making treatment became popular, suddenly any Tom Dick and Harriet could put permanent ink into your brows.

Poorly trained therapists would offer a quick on-the-day consultation and perform the treatment then and there. They charged half the price of other, better qualified, therapists; and this often resulted in irreversible bad jobs.

I've seen women with black slugs permanently arched in surprise. Even after two years they still looked ridiculously dark. Others have had blue or red-looking brows, where the colour had not been mixed correctly. Not to mention the ladies who have incurred infection from the treatment being carried out wrongly.

There used to be a salon in Bath that specialised in semi-permanent make-up. Clients would ask my opinion on this establishment, and one of the things I would suggest was that they look at the work the therapists had had done on themselves. I would explain that, if you went to a tattoo artist and saw that they had the most poorly inked tattoos you had ever seen, you wouldn't trust them to do yours, would you?

They would come back and say, "The therapists looked scary with their unnatural black eyebrows and red-rimmed lips. I definitely wouldn't let them put ink into my skin." My job was done, without me having to bad mouth any salons.

Eyebrow shapes are a big responsibility and important to get right. You must take your time as, unfortunately, any mishap can be a disaster. It takes time for you to get good at this treatment, and we are all on a learning curve when we first start out.

One day, my young therapist – who was known for producing wonderfully shaped eyebrows, suddenly came rushing out of the room in tears. "What's wrong", I said. Between sobs she told me, "I've really messed-up, Wendy! I was waxing and I didn't notice a thin, stringy piece of wax going across the other part of the eyebrow. When I pulled the wax off, the stringy bit pulled the hair out of the wrong place. And now the lady has a whole chunk of hair missing from the middle of her eyebrow." Blowing her nose, she added, "and she's getting married tomorrow!"

This was certainly not a good time to cock-up a treatment. I left my young therapist to calm down and went to talk to the bride-to-be. Yes, indeed she had a chunk missing. Luckily, this lady was very understanding. I finished tidying her brows and gave her an eyebrow make-up kit to patch them up the next day. Then I offered her a free massage as well.

Another thing to remember when shaping a brow is, most importantly, it's about what the client wants. Some people like thick brows, some like ultra-thin, and some like just the hair between the brows taken away to avoid a mono brow. Some want you to help them decide the best shape for them, while others know exactly what they want.

One of my young therapists came out of the treatment room one day demanding, "You need to talk to this woman, Wendy!" She went on to explain, in her opinion, this lady wanted too much hair taken away, and it was going to be ridiculously thin and wouldn't suit her.

When I went into the treatment room the client was fuming. She told me she wanted her eyebrows thin, and the young therapist had basically been arguing with her about taking that much hair off the brow. So, the client told her to go and get the boss. I apologised and finished the treatment giving the client an ultra-thin brow.

Afterwards I sat my prodigy down and told her she was there to do what the client wanted and not what she wanted. Yes, the eyebrow was thin, but it was what the client wanted so it was what the client got, even though it might look strange to us.

Staying with eyes, I remember one eyelash treatment that didn't go well either. When tinting, you mix the pigment with peroxide which activates the colour. After you have prepared the eye area you apply the product for the required time. You then stay with the client to make sure there is no irritation. I often give a hand massage during this time, just to make the treatment more relaxing.

The lady I was treating had medium coloured lashes, and I had applied the darkest tint. When it was time, we removed the product, only to realise there was no colour change. We reapplied the product a second time, but still no change. So, I remixed the product a third time, apologising to the lady. After taking off the product for the third time there was still no change.

I told her I didn't understand why there was no change in colour, and perhaps there was something wrong with the product. I didn't want to apply more to her eyes as they would become irritated. She left the salon, obviously without charge, and I was mystified as this had never happened to me before.

When I went back to tidy the room after an exceptionally long day, I suddenly realised I had mixed the tint with the eyelash cleanser instead of the peroxide. The bottles were almost identical. I couldn't believe I had made such a rookie mistake. I told my colleagues and they were in hysterics.

Nails don't always go to plan either. Sometimes this is because the client's expectations are unreasonable. We can only work with what we have. If you have a very small nail plate (the part of your nail that sits on the finger tip), and no free edge (the nail that grows beyond the finger and gives it length), you can't have a nail extension that is too long.

If you had a long nail extension it would be like an uneven seesaw, and the attached end would not be able to support the length. This will cause the long, free edge of the extension to snap and break.

We always try to be honest with the client and recommend what is best for them. But some people don't listen, and they are often the first clients to return and complain.

On more than one occasion, after explaining all the above, the client has still insisted on having too much length on the extension. Only to return screaming blue murder about how much they had paid for the treatment, how careful they had been, and it could only be the application that was the problem. It was obviously the see-saw effect (that I had taken great pains to warn them about at the time of their treatment) that had caused the breakages. I'm the first one to put my hand up when I get it wrong, but I refuse to accept the blame when it's not my fault.

Then there are the self-tan disasters which are the one thing everyone knows about and are often documented by photographs on the internet. The sit-com,

Friends, showed us a perfect example of tanning going wrong. Remember when Ross got his spray tan and ended up with three Number Two's?

This is certainly a good example of lack of communication between a therapist and client. You must state the obvious clearly to your client. Otherwise you might walk in to find they have put the disposable thongs on their heads.

I'm not joking! On more than one occasion I've walked into the spray room to find my client standing there, stark-naked with the paper pants on their head.

Spray tanning is an art, and my husband reckoned I could probably spray paint a car; I was that good at it. Like any good paint job, the most important part of a spray tan is the preparation. You must make sure your clients know how to prep their skin prior to their appointment. So, pre-tan instructions were a must for a good finish.

In my salon, with every booking, we would advise exactly how to exfoliate to remove any dry, dead skin the night before the treatment. This is done to help avoid the tan sticking to any dry flaky areas and over-darkening. It also helps the tan to last longer as well as helping it to shed evenly. We would also recommend they moisturise any dry areas thoroughly after they exfoliated.

The day of their tanning treatment we asked them not to shower or have any hair removal treatments, including shaving. We would also ask them not to use any type of deodorant and wear loose, baggy, dark clothes to go home in after the spray session.

A classic example of the results of shaving before a spray tan was a bride who had a trial session with us previously and was happy with the result. But she didn't stick to the pre-tanning advice for her wedding spray. She shaved just before her spray session and so ended up with vertical stripes down her legs after she washed off the guide colour.

She got away with it on her wedding day as she wore a full-length dress. But she didn't get the desired effect she wanted for her honeymoon. Her new husband thought she looked like a zebra rather than super sexy.

I used to love the clients who would point-blank tell me that they hadn't put any moisturiser on their legs that morning. Then we would both watch the spray running like a burst pipe down their legs, instead of sticking as it should.

Even though they denied using moisturiser, after we sent them home to shower thoroughly, like magic, the spray would stick evenly to their legs. There was always a sheepish look from them at this point.

Yes, we apply some moisturiser to certain areas, but we do it only when and where it's required to avoid the tan catching and being too dark. For instance, on very dry heals or knees. Remember you come to us because we know what we are doing.

Client: "I have green armpits!"

Me: "You wore deodorant."

Client: "No I didn't."

Me: "OK, you can have a free tan next time."

Surprise, surprise, there was no green underarms the second time, because they now understood why we say no deodorant.

Eventually we wised up and improved our pre-booking procedure to the point of it taking as long as the appointment did. We had to explain what to do pre-tan and spell out the reasons why. We also made it perfectly clear that if the tan didn't take as it should because pre-tan steps were not followed correctly, they would not be getting a further free treatment.

Baggy clothes to go home in were part of our after-tan advice, given at the same time as they booked the appointment. There was always the young girl that had ignored us... as we watched her pulling on her skin-tight jeans, rubbing off the tan that was required to stay on for at least 12 hours.

The spray tan didn't stain your clothes, but it was advisable not to wear white as it would seep through. We also advised no super-sexy designer underwear, as it could stain the elastic.

We had one lady who had the treatment every other week and was so expert at getting tanned she would go home in her old bath robe to prevent any mishaps. Now, she was a pro!

Rain was not great with self-tan either. On more than one occasion we could be seen running up the road with umbrellas over our clients, making sure they didn't get wet, while we got soaked.

Tanning was an art and some therapists and salons just didn't have it. I've had so many people walking through my door shouting for help after another salon had completely messed up their tan. Of course, they had all paid half the price we charged, which meant the salon probably hadn't used a quality product. They would be anything from every shade of mud to all shades of orange.

One therapist had sprayed the palms of the lady's hands, making her look like she had brown gloves on in the middle of the summer. Or the toes that had been saturated with tan, making them look like they had dipped them in chocolate. That client wouldn't be wearing sandals for a while. Streaky bits, dark bits and bits completely missed - you name it, I've seen it.

If a client had been experimenting at home with the latest product, then fair enough. But the poor people who went to a salon expecting a professional tan and came away looking like an Oompa Loompa from Willy Wonka's Chocolate Factory… my heart went out to them.

Sometimes, we could help with a little patching up here and there, but most of the time they just had to cover up and grin and bear it until it wore off.

I started offering fake tanning in the 90's when suddenly it was cool to have a tan, and everyone realised how dangerous sunbathing could be. Even sun beds, once deemed the great alternative, were now recognised to be just as bad, if not worse for the skin.

So, now we had these amazing, new self-tan products that gave you a natural sun-kissed glow without the need to bathe in tea like you had to in the forties. The trouble was you would never know whether you were going to end up golden brown or a ghastly shade of orange.

My first real dabble with applying self-tan was in the spa, and we used a

Clarins product. Back then, there just wasn't anything out there that could guarantee a great colour. It all depended on the person's skin and melanin content. I was always honest and would tell the client, "You may go golden brown or you may go ginger." Not said quite like that, but that was the gist of it.

The other problem with these creams was that they had no guide colour, so you couldn't see where you had applied the product. The best way of not missing any areas was by touch; in other words, the therapist feeling where she had applied the cream. So, for the sake of a guaranteed, even coverage for my clients I applied the product without gloves on. I remember spending a whole summer trying not to expose my orange palms when out socialising, as they looked completely ridiculous.

For these reasons and more, it was a great relief when St Tropez brought out a self-tan product that had a guide colour you could see as you applied it, so no missed areas. It also had a green pigment which guaranteed you would not be any shade of orange.

All the stars were using it, and as a top hotel spa, we got it in. The company came along to train all the staff on the, "new amazing product", and its convoluted application.

One weekday, when the hotel wasn't busy, we spent a morning practising on each other; exfoliating the skin, applying the cream, and then buffing off the excess product. The idea was that the client was able to walk out the door with a ready colour, while the cream worked with the melanin in the skin to produce a bronze kissed look that would last at least a week.

They were right about the lovely colour the skin went, as well as the length of time the tan lasted. It was, however, debateable about the colour you walked out with. Clients often looked more like they had rolled in green cow's muck.

The morning of our training was a success. The problem came when we realised, we had to work in the afternoon looking rather muddy. At the time, our uniform was a tight-fitting, white dress. Inadvertently, some of the brown/green stuff had rubbed off onto our dresses.

But things got even worse as the afternoon wore on. We were performing treatments and getting hot and a little sweaty. This caused the brown mud-like cream to seep through our dresses, making it look like we hadn't washed for a week. On the plus side though, our teeth looked bright white as our faces got darker by the hour.

The hotel manager was less than pleased when he saw the state of his professional therapists and questioned why we had left the product on, rather than washing it off. Our excuse was that we needed to see how the product worked, and what the final colour would be on different people. Secretly, we all wanted to leave it on as it seemed like a good way of getting a free tan.

St Tropez changed the self-tan industry for the better and today it's still one of the top self-tan companies. They were one of the first companies to produce the spray tan, which was revolutionary, and is generally what everyone goes for nowadays.

Some of my younger clients, back in the late 90's, experimented with internet-ordered pills that supposedly produced a tan. These were neither licensed nor safe. They were causing all kinds of health issues and, hopefully, I persuaded these girls not to go down that road again, as they could permanently damage their health.

Today there are still tanning tablets available on the internet, as well as at well-known chemists and health food stores. Some of these tablets are more to do with sun protection rather than tanning, but there are still some that can produce a tan on the skin.

The stronger tablets that claim to produce a tan often contain an ingredient called Canthaxanthin, which is a natural carotene-based additive used to colour food. Although FDA approved for use in food, it's not approved for use in tanning products where it's used in much larger quantities.

This ingredient colours your skin, but the results vary from a golden brown to a yellow orange. There can also be some nasty side effects: nausea, diarrhoea, severe itching, eye problems and even liver damage. The research continues into these types of products, and I'm sure one day they will be perfectly safe for people to use.

The next big thing might be a pill or injections which will tan us the desired colour, while protecting us from skin cancer, and even keep us slim and attractive in the process. We can hope!

What we do for a tan is criminal. Before we bought our salon, and were just employees, we had a sunbed in it. It was a fast tanning, stand-up monstrosity.

There were so many people who were addicted to a tan and used these machines excessively. We kept record cards of how often they were using the machines and for how many minutes. We had strict guidelines we followed. We would only let someone use the machine every 48 hours, but people still overdid the tanning and would go to other salons to get a daily fix.

We would always turn very fair and ginger people away; much to their annoyance. We explained that they would just damage their skin, probably burning before tanning if they were likely to tan at all. We would warn them that they had a higher risk of skin cancer in the future if they tried to tan their skin. We knew these people would just pop off somewhere else for their fix. But at least we had done our bit to try and save them.

I saw so many people get skin cancer in their thirties and forties. These people were often terminally ill, and full of regret for having used these beds. It was the saddest thing ever… losing their lives just to look 'good'.

The first thing we did as soon as we bought the salon was to get rid of the stand-up sunbed.

Ladies, gentlemen & in-between

When I started out all those years ago, I treated mainly ladies, but as time went on, men would become a big part of my clientele. Initially, it was in the spa where a massage was an essential part of a relaxing weekend away from London for every man.

As the years went by, more and more men started to look after themselves, and the Metrosexual was born. This was a man that took interest in his skincare and wanted to maintain and enhance his looks.

This was encouraged through celebrity culture. Footballers and film stars suddenly started to share tips on beautifying themselves. It emerged that these men didn't have naturally gorgeous looking eyebrows after all. They were plucked and shaped to look that good, but previously it had been a well-kept secret.

The cosmetic companies suddenly jumped on the bandwagon, and there were many new product lines being launched just for men. It was no longer just a case of splashing the Brut aftershave on and settling for that.

This was good news for men, as they can also suffer from all kinds of skin problems. At one time their only option was to steal the wife's facial cream and they would never have dared visit a beauty therapist.

Nowadays men can have facials and seek help with all their skin-care problems. They have manicures, pedicures, and enjoy relaxing treatments as much as the ladies.

My son was brought up to look after his skin, and he knew from an early age that you didn't clean your face with soap and water. He now ships his products in from the internet in bulk, and I love him for wanting to look after himself.

Most ladies these days, expect their men to keep themselves groomed and looking good. Most male beauty treatments booked are often heavily influenced by the females in their life.

Often, hair removal on men is seen as a new fashion trend but, in fact, history tells us differently. For example, cavemen removed their hair for survival. They didn't wash back then, and this led to their hair emitting a foul odour which would scare away the prey. Also, the hair on the body would make a great home for itchy parasites. They would use flint or shells to remove their unwanted hair.

The Egyptians saw facial hair on men as uncivilized, and if you look at a painting of the ancient male, you will notice there is little or no body hair. This is certainly an indication that they liked a smooth body.

Changing times and changing fashions meant the Elizabethan man favoured a beard. Whereas more recently in the 60's and 70's hair and the natural look was all the rage.

Present day hair trends were started by sportsmen. Athletes, bodybuilders, cyclists, and swimmers all remove their body hair. The latter two for comfort and performance, and the bodybuilder for looks and the ability to show off muscles.

It's popular nowadays to have designer stubble on the face, rather than a full beard. This is deemed sexy and attractive. Likewise, hair on certain parts of the body is more acceptable than on others. For instance, well-kept hair on the chest is seen as sexy, but excessively hairy hands are just too gorilla-like.

In the 90's a hairy back suddenly became a big no-no. Some men were glad of this, especially in the hot weather. A hairy back or chest can become extremely uncomfortable and rather itchy in the heat.

Out came the razors, but just like women, men soon realised there was a constant upkeep to shaving, and the re-growth was itchy and uncomfortable. The new Metrosexual man needed a saviour, and he turned to me, the beauty therapist.

Suddenly, it was the norm for me to be waxing chests, backs and even arms. I also treated the cyclists, who had previously shaved. They would book appointments for a full-body wax, which was a long job, hard work and a tad painful for them.

One time, there were a group of professional rugby players who turned up ready for their new member to have his back and chest waxed for a hot date the following night. They stopped off for his treatment on their way to play golf.

They all piled in the door with the young chap. I had a reception full of older ladies sitting in awe at these unexpected visitors. This most certainly brightened up their normal Saturday morning appointments.

"Can we come in with him, he is very nervous?" They raucously asked. "It's just for moral support"

"No!" I said emphatically. "There's not enough room for you lot, besides, you really don't have to worry, I'll look after him."

They pleaded, asking for just one or two of them to go in with him. But I wasn't going to have any of them in the room. I didn't trust them not to misbehave, so I stuck to my guns. I told them they could all wait outside the salon and warned them to leave my ladies in peace.

The poor newbie team member was rather glad that I had refused entry to his teammates as he didn't trust any of them either. I took him in the room, put him at ease and started his waxing.

The salon was not left in peace. The car horn was blowing periodically outside and lots of good-natured banter could be heard. I just carried on with the treatment and hoped my ladies were taking it in good spirit.

Halfway through the waxing the man's phone started ringing. "They want to know how long I will be" the young chap said. "Tell them about twenty minutes." I replied.

Five-minutes later the phone was ringing again. Now bear in mind, I was a little bit older than this lad, though not old enough to be his mother. This made me feel protective. I also knew a first-time wax can be an unpleasant and often painful experience. As a professional I wanted to make it as comfortable as possible for him.

"Give me the phone." I said, which he happily did. "Now listen to me! If you keep interrupting me this will take a lot longer. You all want to go off and play golf as quickly as possible, so let me get on with it." I told the rugby star on the other end of the line.

At which point he very politely asked if he could come in and get the car keys.

"Oh alright… yes a quick in and out." I told him.

This very nice-looking and polite young chap knocked and came in, apologising for his teammate's behaviour and for disturbing me. He had a quick reassuring chat to the lad while I carried on with the wax, and then disappeared from the room, presumably with the car keys.

With no further interruptions I finished quickly. Giving the man some aftercare advice and some soothing lotion, then I left him to get dressed.

I went to the reception and sorted the bill on the computer while looking out at the rugby players all staring in the window and giggling like children. Luckily, all the ladies in the salon were taking this onslaught in good humour.

So, I waited for about ten minutes, and slowly the door opened, and the lad's head peered out of the room. "Sorry about this." He said as he gingerly approached the desk. To all my ladies delight he was only wearing his boxer shorts and a pair of trainers. "He stole my clothes when he took the keys." He explained very red faced.

The car horn was beeping, the guys were all laughing and cheering, and my ladies were smiling from ear-to-ear as this muscular young rugby player made good his escape rather quickly from the salon.

I had a lot of regular male clients for chest and back waxing over the years. There was always good banter while the treatment went on.

One of them springs to mind. He was an Italian man, with whom I had a real laugh. We got to know each other very well over his regular back and chest wax. He was very good-looking and was a terrible flirt. I liked him, but knew he was a bit of a lad. The more I got to know him, the more interested he became in me.

When one day he found out I had separated from my first husband the flirting became much more obvious. He really started to make a play for me.

He would promise me lovely homemade Italian food accompanied by red wine and candlelight if I went on a date with him. I knew I should have put a stop to this kind of flirtation, but at an incredibly sad and uncertain time in my life, he lifted my spirits and made me feel attractive.

However, tempted I was to go out with him, I knew it wouldn't be a good idea. So, I told him very gently no, putting an end to this little flirtation. Or so I thought. The problem was that I had unprofessionally allowed this flirtation to start, and he didn't want it to end. He even got hold of my mobile phone number and started calling me. I had to stop treating him before he finally got the message.

He still came to the salon booking his treatments with other therapists though. He was just as flirty with them; it was in his nature. But I do believe he really had a soft spot for me, and always had a hopeful twinkle in his eye whenever he saw me. Or maybe he was just after a lifetime of free waxing?

As with everything in the industry, things develop, and different treatments become popular. Ladies had been having their Brazillian and Hollywood waxes for some time and suddenly they were saying, "Well, if I'm neat, tidy and hair-free down below, then so can my man be."

The sex industry and pornography were also influencing what was the norm for the younger generation. Men suddenly had either extraordinarily little pubic hair or none. Even mainstream, if you watched any nude scene on a film there were certainly no hairy bums on the men.

Thus, the male bikini wax was born. It was known as the Back, Sack & Crack Wax. I've always liked a challenge, and this was certainly the next one for me.

Initially, there were no courses to go on for this type of waxing. As far as I was concerned, I was qualified in waxing and this was just another area to wax.

With the help of one of my young therapist's boyfriend as a model, both she and I developed a good procedure. He was a nice Italian man, who looking back, was an awfully brave volunteer. It couldn't have been easy to have two of us staring at his private parts while he was lying on our couch in a disposable thong.

We spent a considerable amount of time working out what the best positions were going to be for us to get a good result. We also needed to work out what part of his anatomy he needed to pull back and hold, and what part we needed to stretch.

We eagerly applied the wax to his groin, his balls, his legs, and his bum. If he ever reads this, he will know who he is. It was all done tongue in cheek while having a laugh, but it was still painful for him. I'm sure we thanked him, but hey, thank you again!

Suddenly, our little pink salon was offering male Brazillian waxing, and we did quite a lot of them initially. Did I like performing the treatment? Well yes and no, really.

I liked the challenge and enjoyed perfecting a good treatment; a job well done. But I never really got comfortable with waxing a man's balls. No matter how you stretched and pulled the area you could see the pain in their eyes, which always made me cringe. The area was left pink and rather haggard looking afterwards which didn't help my appreciation of the male anatomy one little bit.

After one such wax, I had a dream. Well it was more like a nightmare. In the dream the man had come back crying to me the day after his treatment. "Look what you've done!" He opened his hands and he had his balls in his palms. "They fell off!" He said.

I woke up in a cold sweat. It had felt a little too real for my liking.

After about a year, we stopped advertising the male Brazillian and it slowly filtered out. There were still a lot of bum waxes, but bottoms didn't worry me. I just preferred to stay away from the balls.

We used to have lots of gay guys coming into the salon. This was something that became the norm as time went on. Both men and women became much more open about their sexuality. I had so many openly gay men whom I just loved treating. They would know everything about the latest treatments and products, often more than many women.

Stevie sashayed into the salon wearing his denim hot pants and his bright-red patent wellies declaring, "I need my bum and legs waxed. I'm off to *Gay Pride* next week and I can't look like a *He-Man*." This perfectly turned out guy could have had hair down to his toes and he would never have looked like a He-anything, he was positively stunning.

Sometimes, you had the men come in who had a gay or feminine side that they were exploring. One such chap was married, but he would ask me about having his eyelashes and brows tinted. "Do you think anyone would notice?" He would ask.

Or, while waxing his brows he would mention that he wanted them shaped more feminine, but not so feminine that his wife would notice. He would ring and book an appointment for a manicure as early in the day as possible, explaining he liked to wear coloured nail polish but needed to remove it before he returned home that evening.

It became very apparent that his wife didn't like him coming to the salon and he had to keep a lot of the treatments he had quiet. I don't know what became of him, but I hope he was eventually able to be honest with his wife.

I experienced and saw so many men who were confused about their gender. Once they trusted me, they would be honest about their plight. Sometimes, it was sad that they were constantly fighting with society, family or just their own conscience to be who they really were.

Pete arrived one Saturday morning asking if we could fit him in for a manicure and pedicure in the afternoon. Testing the waters, he asked if we would apply coloured nail polish as well. Of course, we would.

Once he realised, we were normal, friendly people he said, "Just so you know, I'll be arriving as Petra this afternoon. Is this a problem for you?" No, it wasn't a problem for us. He was most welcome as Pete or Petra.

He arrived very smartly dressed in a skirt and jacket with a lovely blonde wig and a smart pair of court shoes. His make-up was applied rather well, and in fact, it was better than I had seen on some women.

We spent a nice afternoon with Petra. He explained that as an older aged man with a successful business, a wife of 40 years, children, and grandchildren, he couldn't openly indulge in the joy he got from dressing as a woman. So, two or three times a year he would travel a considerable distance to where he was not known and have a weekend of being Petra.

He was such a lovely man, and we enjoyed his company that afternoon immensely. He had come to terms with his double life and accepted that he had to hide the other side of himself whilst at home. Perhaps, if he had been born nowadays things would be different, as society is much more accepting of people's choices now.

Some people would know a transgender or a transsexual person straight away. I haven't always noticed. A person is just a person to me, and I never assume anything about anybody. Just the other day I was gazing at a man, thinking how attractive he was. I couldn't put my finger on why I was drawn to him. Then I realised he was wearing false eyelashes. They looked rather pretty.

We had a beautiful lady who had a regular back massage in the salon, and she was stunning. Her make-up, hair and nails were all immaculate. She was the type of woman you would admire walking down the street.

I mentioned how quiet and shy she was one day to a colleague. I was told maybe that was because she was transgender and was sensitive.

I hadn't even realised and couldn't believe it. My colleague pointed out a few details such as her Adam's apple and hands; things I hadn't even noticed because everything else had been so petite about her.

Another chap came for an eyebrow shape, and he was a real tough looking guy. He looked like he had just stepped off a building site. He had booked an eyebrow shape which was quite the norm for lots of men by this time in my career.

I asked him, "How would you like your eyebrows shaped?" He responded, "A high arch and as feminine as possible."

I hid my surprise, as he really didn't look feminine at all. Once we started chatting, his female side came out, and it turned out that he was a transvestite.

Another time, we kept getting phone calls asking for advice about make-up. The guy would ask me, "Which colour eye shadow is better for a man, blue or grey?"

Over the telephone this was a difficult question. Was this man serious or just someone trying to lead us up the garden path? Was he trying to tell me something, or inadvertently asking about coming out? I didn't know, so I needed to be sensitive as I didn't want to cause him any distress.

I said that it would depend on the occasion, and what else he would be wearing. This same man called about three times asking different questions on make-up, eyelash tints, eyebrow shaping and applying false eyelashes. Each time he called I gave him honest advice and suggested he came in for a proper chat and a make-up lesson. I hoped he would realise we were a non-judgmental salon and we would gladly help him. But he never booked an appointment.

One day a guy walked in wearing men's clothes but with a feminine twist. He wore a rather attractive flowery purple shirt with buttons on the left, and a scarf draped around his shoulders. He was also wearing some light make-up.

He came in asking if we could do a third piercing in his ear, which we gladly did for him. We chatted during the treatment and he never said he had contacted us before, but I recognised his voice as the man on the phone. He only ever came in the once and he was a nice chap. I hope he was able to work himself out.

I sometimes think what great courage people have for being who they are, especially those who are not the norm in our society. I was always honoured that people felt comfortable in our non-judgmental salon and loved to help them experiment with their look and the person they wanted to be.

I often think about how our society demands men to dress and look a certain way and women another. I think men have drawn the short straw on this one. As women, we have far more choice in the clothes we can wear, how we have our hair done, and the wonderful paint we wear on our faces. Men are much more restricted in how they are meant to dress and look.

From meeting so many different people over the years, I've learnt one overriding thing. People are not their clothes, make-up, or hairstyle. They are who they are on the inside, deep in their soul. The outer part is just the shell which is decorated and adorned to look the way we want ourselves and others to see us.

On the whole

Holistic medicine and holistic beauty are similar. They both work on the principle of treating the whole person. It's all about looking at the root cause to stop the problem, rather than just treating the symptoms.

A perfect example of this is when someone comes to me with a skin concern. I would ask questions about everything: their diet, exercise, stress levels, working environment, as well as their home skin-care regime. All these factors play a role in healthy skin.

Maybe they are using an inappropriate product or exposing their skin to an aggravator without realising it. But it could just as easily be stress having a direct effect on the skin; causing spots, pimples, redness, or flaking. Improving a skin problem can, and often does, mean making some lifestyle changes.

Holistic treatments work on balancing the body and the spirit; looking at all the systems of the body, including the ones we can't see.

As a new therapist I never had a clue about holistic treatments. When I began my training in the eighties, we didn't discuss any alternative therapies apart from aromatherapy. We only discussed diet and the effect on the skin. We never touched on anything remotely spiritual or any kind of therapy that dealt with energy fields or rebalancing them.

The only time alternative treatments were mentioned was in our third year of training. A very hippy lady came in and demonstrated reflexology and we all thought she was away with the fairies. My peers laughed at the thought of putting pressure on certain parts of the foot to balance the inner systems of the body. I had a slightly different view from my own past experiences, but I kept them to myself. I was young at the time and didn't want to appear different.

Growing up, my grandparents had a different outlook to life than most. My grandmother read the cards as well as tea leaves. She believed in nature and had a strong spiritual side to her. She celebrated the seasons and revelled in the power of them. She liked nothing more than going to the seaside on a cold stormy day and, "washing the cobwebs from her mind", as she put it. She could often feel things about others and believed in spirits and the afterlife. She was known as the white witch of the family.

My granddad, who called me, "Wednesday", also had a spiritual side. I had a connection to him that I could never quite explain but he always knew what I was thinking and feeling.

I suffered from warts on my hands as a child, and my grandfather would place his hands on them, and they would disappear. This was always after countless trips to the doctor and different medications. He would often place his hands on someone in pain and it would go away. If you met him, you would never have known he had this amazing ability as he was a salt of the Earth kind of chap and laughed at everything. He never considered this to be any type of special gift. It just was.

When I was a young adult, I would often feel things about a person or place; and it wasn't always pleasant feelings either. I found it all rather scary, so I blocked these feeling from an early age, deciding I didn't want to go there. Little did I know that going into the beauty industry would lead me down a path that was similar to both of my grandparents.

Please don't think I'm saying I'm some kind of magical healer, as my granddad was. But by holding the intention of wanting to help, I found that I could adjust my therapy, so that my clients got the maximum benefit from the treatments. They would often leave with a headache gone or feeling less anxious and more peaceful.

As a therapist, when you place your hands on someone, you enter their personal space. You soon start to realise it's not just their flesh you feel, but their energy, too. It comes in the form of a tingle, a heated hand or sometimes just a feeling. When your client becomes very relaxed and comfortable with you, they often open up. This happens, not only on a conscious level, but also on a subconscious one. Very soon into my career I knew I was feeling more than just skin when I was massaging people.

When performing a relaxing treatment on someone I would often know if they had a headache or if they were unhappy. I wanted to help them, and I suppose I wanted to heal them. I also wanted all my clients to have, not just a good treatment, but an amazing one. So, I would put all my thoughts and energy into every client. They all received my heart and soul every time I was with them. Of course, the more I put into them, the more I felt from them.

Not all therapists gave it their all in this way. Many of my colleagues merely went through the motions. They never thought for a moment how wonderful they wanted to make these people feel. Maybe they had too much on their own minds to think of others. Though their clients enjoyed the treatments, there was never that wow factor that was so important for me to give.

About the same time that I started working in the spa, treatments such as Indian head massage and reflexology were becoming popular. I began to take an interest in them and read up on the history. Although to the Western world these were relatively new treatments, they went back thousands of years in the East.

I met a therapist who performed Reiki. She was an Australian girl who had learned this skill, and it was still very much an unknown treatment in the UK. I wanted to learn more about energy.

Why did my hands get so hot when I touched painful areas on my clients?

Why did I feel their emotions?

Why did I walk away with the same symptoms as they complained of?

Why did I feel like there was a wall in front of some people I treated?

Talking to her really piqued my interest in holistic therapies and I found myself booked on to an Indian head massage course. This really opened my eyes to alternative beliefs about systems of the body that could not be seen or were not recognised by science.

I was suddenly looking into the age-old beliefs of Indian and Chinese cultures; that we are more than just our physical selves. It's widely believed we have systems in the body that are unseen, that have a direct effect on our energy levels and health.

The chakras are one system not seen in any Western anatomy book. These are likened to vortexes, spinning life energy into or out of our bodies. These wheels are scattered through our body, and if left out of balance, they can contribute to physical illness. As a holistic therapist I work on balancing this and other unseen systems.

There are also meridians, or energy points throughout our bodies like electric wiring. This wiring can become blocked and by using pressure point massage it's believed you can release stagnant energy. This helps us feel more energised, balanced, and healthier.

Our Aura is a proven energy field that surrounds our body. It is believed to be made up of colours and reading them is believed to help us identify emotional and physical health problems.

Some people say that all these things I've mentioned are nonsense. But working on these unseen systems over three decades has proved to me without a doubt that they exist. Focusing on them during treatments can have a surprisingly profound result for the client, and I've witnessed this first-hand on many occasions.

The downside of connecting with people on this deeper level soon became apparent to me. It could be an emotionally draining experience, and I would often walk out of the treatment feeling completely shattered. Sometimes I would even feel the same negative symptoms as the person I was working on.

I remember once leaving the room after giving a lovely lady a massage treatment. I felt like someone was sitting on my chest and was struggling to catch my breath. The lady in question came into the reception area looking very refreshed and explained that she had not felt this good in weeks. She had had some bad asthma attacks recently which involved trips to the hospital. She said, "It feels like a weight has been lifted from my chest."

There were so many people who had headaches at the start of the treatment, only to be relieved at the end, not realising that I had somehow taken their terrible headache on myself.

Tiredness was a huge pain for me in my early days of being a therapist. I could put my hands on someone and feel an overwhelming sense of wanting to go to sleep. When talking to the client it would turn out they were having problems sleeping for various reasons. Or they were just having an exhausting time in their life.

During my Indian head massage course, I finally learned the basic principles of protecting myself against all this negative energy and my client's pain. I now knew how to ground myself and put up a protective shield.

Grounding is a way of keeping your connection to the here and now. One way of doing this is by imagining your feet are like tree roots connected and penetrating deep into the earth. The earth's natural energy field will keep you stable and connected to the here and now while carrying out a treatment.

Protecting yourself is an intention to not take on negativity and bad health. This is done by taking the time to imagine a protective field around you like a bubble. The more you practice this form of meditation, the stronger your force field becomes.

The biggest problem was, and is, fitting in these protection rituals with back to back clients. You really must keep reminding yourself how important protection is. Going home feeling worn out and poorly can be a good reminder to take the time you need before treatments to protect yourself from other people's negative energy.

I've often been seen nipping to the loo before a treatment. I would stand eyes closed, palms out, practicing my protection procedure and grounding techniques. It would have looked a peculiar sight if anyone ever saw me. Why the loo? Because it was often the only quiet space in a busy salon.

To this day, if I know I'm going into a potentially toxic environment, I take the time to do a little protective meditation and ground myself.

Unexplained happenings

It seemed a natural step to train in Reiki which I found great, especially for helping me perfect my self-protection skills. It also enabled me to understand the tingling and hot hands I got when I was giving treatments. And it explained the thoughts that would come to me mid-treatment about a client. Most of all, it helped me understand the healing ability everyone has within them.

At this point I would like to say that I am not someone who goes around touching people and talking about their energy. In fact, I'm the most unintuitive person in the world mostly.

All kinds of people have told me at one time or another that I have an aura indicating that I'm a healer and a spiritual person. I personally think that we all have this ability; especially women, as we often have a maternal instinct to love, heal and protect. I think in today's world, which is all about proof and science, it's easy to forget that simply to feel the energy of love is healing in itself.

What is Reiki? Here is the dictionary definition:

A healing technique based on the principle that the therapist can channel energy into the patient by means of touch, to activate the natural healing processes of the patient's body and restore physical and emotional well-being.

As I said, I am not a healer. To me, Reiki is about the power of love & compassion and having the intention to make someone feel better in themselves.

Do you remember the feeling of tranquillity you felt when your mum would smooth your head when you were little? Or when a nurse puts a reassuring hand on your shoulder during a worrying time in a hospital bed? Everyone knows how wonderful a friend's embrace is when they are feeling low. These are all examples of the positive power of touch.

So as soon as I heard about Reiki I signed-up for my Reiki 1 Attunement, not really knowing what attunement was or what to expect. But I just knew it was for me.

This Reiki 1 course was all about working on oneself, friends, and family. We would be required to complete our Reiki 2 course before we could carry out the treatment on paying clients though. There was a gap between the two so we could heal, practice, and build our own positive energy.

There were eight of us on the course from all walks of life: therapists, a grandmother, a housewife and a builder. Our Reiki master – the tutor, was a lovely lady and very spiritual. She was an unusual person who believed in god as well as Tarot cards and Reiki. She certainly had all her bases covered in that regard.

We started the day's course with an explanation of the history of the treatment and what Reiki 1 was all about. Basically, it was about switching on our inner ability to channel healing energy from the universe; something that's inherent in all of us but has been lost over the ages.

We were required to heal ourselves, let go of negative energy and forgive those that had hurt us. We cleared our minds of stagnant and negative energy, so that good, positive energy could flow through us and then into others.

After the initial introduction, it was time to learn some meditation. This involves the practise of stilling the mind. The first meditations were guided, so quite easy for my busy mind, and I found them very relaxing.

We then had to work on forgiving others that had hurt us in the past, and we did this by writing a list of the bad things that people had done to us. Then we burnt the list. Indeed, this is done in many cultures and is useful for getting rid of emotional baggage. I loved this idea; especially as forgiving people can be a really hard thing to do. Holding on to hurt and pain depletes our positive energy, so getting rid of it is important. Personally, I think everybody would benefit from building a bonfire and having a weekly burn.

Next was the time to go inside (our minds) and find our Reiki Guide. We did this by meditating in a group. The Master led us towards a healing light, where she left us individually to discover our guiding spirit. The plan was that our new Guide would introduce themselves, and we would spend some time with them before the Master led us back to the here and now.

Well, as I said earlier, I had some spiritual encounters when I was younger that scared me to death, so I was a little apprehensive about this one.

Initially, being guided to the light was lovely and relaxing, but then as we were left in the light to be found by our guide, the fog came down for me. I was looking for light and guides, but all I could see was fog and haze. Typical of me, while I was in my (so say) meditative state… I was also in a bit of a panic… I was asking myself all sorts of questions.

"Was I going to be the only one who didn't get a guide?"

"What was I going to do if I didn't get a one?"

"Would this mean I wouldn't be able to perform Reiki?

"Should I be honest and tell everyone I don't have a guide or just make something up?"

Then suddenly, as the smoky fog cleared, I saw a native American Indian chief standing there looking at me. He was a rather scary, stern looking man in full war-paint and headdress. Despite his fierce appearance, calm came over me, and my mind was still and quiet for once.

I was very relieved to have found him; and it was just in the nick of time, as we were then being guided out of the meditation. I did think my new guide looked a little cross though as I opened my eyes and returned to reality.

The next step was to go around the circle with each of us telling the group about their guides. One lady had a Buddhist monk who held his hands together and bowed to her in a serene way. Another had a Chinese girl who smiled at her sweetly. On it went, my friends for the day telling wonderful stories about gentle, smiling guides. Even the only man in our group got a high priest in a turban who gave him a peaceful look.

It eventually came to my turn and I had to explain that I had seen a rather scary Indian chief who looked very severe with a frown on his face. I laughed and asked why

I didn't get a happy, smiling chap like everyone else. The Master just said, "You get what you need, not what you want."

After lunch we went, one at a time, to be attuned. I sat with my eyes closed while the Master touched me gently on my shoulders and did her thing. It was a weird experience, almost humbling, and made me feel very emotional. It was like a light had been switched on in the deepest part of me.

Once we were all attuned, we paired up to practise on each other. With this treatment your hands mostly hover just above the body. You start from the head and move down to the feet. The palm of your hands become very tingly, like electric is running through them. And they heat up; more so in certain areas where there may be pain and discomfort. It was the weirdest feeling and sometimes your hands would get so hot it felt like they were burning.

I was practising on a fellow student, and it wasn't just my hands getting hotter and hotter, but my back was burning up as well. The heat ran from the top of my head all down my back, getting hotter and hotter as I carried out the treatment.

The Reiki master suddenly said to me, "Is your back feeling hot?" "Yes, how did you know?" I said. "Your chief is standing right behind you." "Shit!" I thought. What's he doing there, that scary man looking over my shoulder?

The teacher then went on to say, "He isn't scary he's just very peaceful. He's here to calm you while you perform your treatment as you're a rather scatty person. You obviously need a little discipline in your treatments and life. Don't worry; he's very friendly, nothing to be afraid of."

I had a wonderful day learning all of this and meeting my Guide, albeit a little bit of a weird one.

As soon as I completed my Reiki 1, I got stuck into practising on everybody – including the dog! One of these was my business partner who had bad arthritis in her knees, which would swell-up and cause her lots of pain. She was originally sceptical of this holistic treatment, but that's the beauty of it – you don't have to believe in it for it to work. She soon realised, that along with a sense of relaxation, her knees felt less painful and the swelling went down after a treatment. Her interest had suddenly peaked.

During one of these treatments she was really relaxed and then suddenly halfway through, she said, "Oh my God Wendy I saw him!" "Saw who?" I said. "Your Indian chief, he was standing right behind you, and he does look scary."

After a while I took the Reiki 2 course to learn about working on paying clients. Reiki 2 was not as profound, but just as interesting. One thing that came from this course was that a client may not always walk away feeling light and wonderful. As I was told before, "you get what you need, not what you want."

We were given an example of this on this second course. A client had come in for a treatment with many health problems. She was a very poorly lady. She had a relaxing Reiki treatment and left with the promise of booking another treatment. She telephoned the practitioner a couple of weeks later, furious.

She declared that after the treatment all she had done was cry and feel angry to the point of shouting and screaming at herself and everyone else. Why didn't she feel better? She wanted to feel happy and calm, not upset and angry.

The practitioner had a long chat with her, and it came about that the anger, frustration and sadness were all things she felt about her body failing her, and she had spent a year not admitting any of these feelings. She just put on a brave face and carried on with life. She was not expressing her emotions and was hiding from her own feelings.

We often see these kinds of emotions as negative, but they only become negative if we hold them in. Expressing them is positive. So, the long and short of it is that the Reiki had a healing effect of enabling her to let out these trapped emotions. Hopefully, helping her to move forward and come to terms with her health issues, and even helping them to heal. As soon as she realised this she booked straight back in for another appointment.

No matter what treatment I was giving, the Reiki energy would often 'switch on' without me asking it to. Other times I needed to switch it on purposively. I did this through a quick meditation with a formal request to switch it on. While I asked for the power to be turned on, I also requested protection and help from my guide.

During the treatments I would get things come into my head. It was often suggestions for the client to look after themselves, or a need to pass on reassurance to them that everything would be OK. Before all my hands-on relaxing treatments, I would always explain to the client that sometimes things came into my head and asked them if they wanted me to tell them. Mostly they did, and I would say something that often meant absolutely nothing to me, but they understood perfectly.

Not everyone thought this was a gift, and in fact a lot of religious people thought it was the Devil at work. One such client was a Baptist minister. On our first meeting she had come straight from administering a funeral with the Australian flag painted on every one of her nails.

My colleague started telling her about the Reiki treatments she had been receiving from me, which was helping with her arthritis. The minister suddenly declared this was, "Evil working through you."

Overhearing the conversation, I asked her why. She told me, in no uncertain terms, that it was the Devil coming through me with his power. I replied that it's just a calming treatment that helps people feel better. "How can this be evil?" I asked. She told me that she was God's disciple, and God talked to her. She said that she went every Sunday to a church where they would heal people, but what I did was non-religious, and it was therefore the Devils work. Apparently, he was just gaining my trust ready to corrupt me, and my clients too.

I wanted to tell her she was being a bit hypocritical, and maybe it was the Devil talking to her and God talking to me. Of course, I didn't, as the beauty salon wasn't the place to have a major discussion on the merits of God and the Devil. Also, she was a client, so I just nodded and took my leave.

I respect the fact that not everyone believes in this type of treatment, but the more I carried out this practice, the more clients left me feeling relieved from both physical and mental pain. I can't call that evil, can you?

On another of her visits we got talking about a ghost we all thought we had in the salon. We told the minister how things would just disappear and after stripping the place and not finding any traces, the missing object would suddenly turn up right where we thought it was in the beginning.

Our naughty little poltergeist showed its mischievousness on more than one occasion. Once, I lost a charm from my bracelet and we looked everywhere to no avail. Then about six months later I walked into the salon first thing in the morning, and my charm was sitting right in the middle of the floor. We would often smell pipe smoke or cigarettes when there was nobody around smoking. This was such a strong smell that we would always check around us to see if someone had lit up in the salon.

The salon used to be a butcher's shop, and one of our therapist's great granddads used to work there. She said that the place where we smelled cigarette smoke would have been the office area. Back in the day, all the butchers would smoke in there. There weren't any health and hygiene rules then.

We put it down to the old butchers keeping an eye on their butcher shop and having a laugh with us girls for doing funny treatments in their old domain.

After telling the Baptist minister all this one day, she announced that she could come in and do an exorcism, declaring how we had to banish this evil from the salon. We gently declined the offer because we honestly thought this was a mischief maker who hadn't ever given us cause to feel uncomfortable. We certainly didn't feel our ghost or ghosts were evil.

As well as Reiki, I was very much into colour therapy. Colour is everywhere and we are surrounded by it our whole lives. It's bound to affect our mind and mood.

The science of colour is interesting, and certain colours are used in hospitals as they are believed to have a calming and healing effect. You never find red paint on their walls as red is a stimulating, sexual and exciting colour. Have a look round next time you go, and you will find pale-blue and yellow colours on the walls. Equally, schools go for certain colours to encourage learning.

When looking into colours, each one represents healing for particular emotional or physical problem. We are drawn to certain colours at different times of our lives. When we look at what those colours represent, we often find they match the healing we need at that time. Again, it's your prerogative to think this a little *away with the fairies*. But I have used colours to great effect over the years.

I would ask my clients to think of a colour while they were having a treatment. This was a great way for them to clear their minds of everyday worries. Afterwards they would tell me which they had chosen. Then I would look it up in my book. Often the colour they had chosen was the colour that represented the issue they were experiencing at the time. I would then suggest they meditate or wear that colour until the problem went away.

Green is for new beginnings and balance, so meditate on it when your relationship with yourself or others is out of whack. Physically, it's supposed to help with angina, heart disease and warts, to name but a few ailments.

Orange is for joy. If you are lacking joy in your life and feel depressed, surround yourself with orange. Also, if you need to let go of past wrongs, orange is your colour. Physical healings are arthritis, colds, constipation, and kidney disease.

So many of my clients would be in wonder that the colour they thought of was the very colour they needed for healing.

I do have some weird and wonderful stories about my holistic treatments, but these stay with me. Some of my clients have had deeply profound and emotional experiences that are not for me to share. All I know is, that it doesn't matter if it was a direct result of the treatment or just the fact that someone wanted to make them feel special. The results myself and my clients have experienced have always been positive.

Never work with children

I love children... but didn't ever imagine working with them when I started out in the beauty industry.

The more popular the beauty industry became, the more mums came to have treatments, and in return the more they decided to treat their little ones. Prior to my high street salon, I didn't really have anything to do with children, apart from my own. When we bought the business, we inherited a pink beauty salon with lots of retail aimed at young girls: hair bands, lip balms, and other pretty paraphernalia, all aimed at youngsters and teenagers.

Because of this, the secondary school girls would invade us after school each day. Mums would also bring their younger girls along on a Saturday to buy some little pretties. I love kids, girls especially, so although this side of the business didn't make much money, it was just nice to be a one-stop girly salon.

Ladies would sometimes walk through the door with a three-year-old in tow apologising because they had no childcare. They had a bikini line wax booked and didn't want to cancel or just not turn up. We were always grateful and never minded the children in the salon.

No-shows are the biggest pain in the behind to any salon or therapist. You have the time and room booked out, you are all set up, and on busy days you have turned other appointments away as well. Then the time comes and goes with no client turning up. It's a waste of money and time, and nothing makes a therapist or a salon owner angrier.

All kinds of ridiculous excuses were used for not turning up. Unless it was a hospital trip or a death in the family, we found it completely unacceptable not to arrive for a booked appointment. No-shows were and are the biggest reason for loss of money in a beauty salon, and I think these people are rude and inconsiderate.

Therefore, the lady that turned up with her children in tow for a ten-pound treatment was more highly regarded than the one that booked a hundred-pound treatment and didn't arrive.

We had clients that thought they were the best clients in the world because they spent a lot of money. They would never understand when we didn't want to take bookings from them anymore as they had let us down too many times.

"But I spend a lot of money here, you should value me." The trouble was that, although we did value them, they didn't value us. They never understood how them letting us down cost us a lot of money.

So, we would welcome ladies who arrived with their children. Some treatments were easier to do with accompanying children than others. To avoid explaining why I was putting hot wax on their mum's plum, we would always offer to take the girls off their hands while they had their treatments. This avoided awkward questions.

The little girls were easy to look after and great fun to entertain. We would paint their nails and cover them with little sparkling gems. If the appointment were a long one, we would also pop their hair up with pretty hair bands.

The little boys were not so easy to entertain; until we discovered they liked a stick-on tattoo of a dragon or cross on their arms. So, we always made sure we had a few of those in stock too. There were also girls who preferred evil looking tattoos and boys who liked their nails painted. It was fun for us as well as the kids, and we always had a grateful mum. The idea for the Fairy Parties was born.

Suddenly, every Saturday, we were holding girl's birthday parties. We were hosting fairy and princess parties for ten or more girls at a time. We had a huge front area that would be turned into a little girl's wonderland for an hour or two.

We would beautify the little one's nails with bright colours and sparkling gems. Next, we would dress their hair by curling it and putting it up using pretty hair bands and clips. Then we would apply appropriate make-up and face art for the girl's ages. Finally, to finish the look, we would go mad with the glitter spray. The music would be on full-blast, and the little ones could even bring their own CD's to have a boogie to.

As we were a working beauty salon, there was no food allowed on the premises, although we did supply a drink and a birthday cake. We would all sing Happy Birthday whilst the birthday girl blew out the candles. The cake would then be cut up and put into party bags, along with some pretty treats for them to take away.

It was two mad hours with party music and lots of girls getting overly excited. It was also good fun to do, and a great money maker. We were suddenly inundated with girls ranging from six to sixteen. Along with the girls came the mums as an adult was required to be present to avoid any legal issues of being left alone with the kids.

Some mums and their daughters are just lovely and really appreciated the effort we put into the parties. But not all of them were so pleasant. Some of the girls were very spoilt; and sometimes the mums could be quite rude and obnoxious. Oh yes, often the mums were worse than their awful offspring. And in fact, I always felt sorry for the children as they couldn't help being spoilt monsters with mums that had made them that way.

Some of the little ones would put you on a pedestal and were so grateful for every little bit of fairy dust we sprinkled on them. They would hold hands and kiss each other dancing around the room. We enjoyed these little cuties so much and would sing and dance with them having as much fun as they did.

It wasn't quite so much fun when we were faced with a group of girls sniggering and whispering to each other, demanding to be the birthday girl's best friend, or leaving another girl out because she wasn't dressed in the right outfit.

Some birthday girls would have a tantrum because they had decided that their friend's nails were a nicer colour than their own. God forbid if a ten-year-old didn't get their hair in a certain way, or if their friends were not done in the right order. The parties were time sensitive, so we couldn't just change hair styles and nail colours because a little girl suddenly declared she didn't want what she had previously chosen.

In all honestly, I think these girls just wanted the party to be perfect for their friends, and the thought of everyone not saying how wonderful it had been was enough to turn the birthday girl into a monster. She often so desperately wanted everyone to love her that she forgot to enjoy herself.

Then there were the teenagers who would be solemn and aloof, leaving you wondering why they had demanded this kind of party in the first place. Maybe it was mum's choice, trying to keep her little girl for longer?

Half the teenage girls would turn their noses up at the treatments on offer, and often refused to have their hair done or their nails painted. They would walk out with a little eyeliner on and a sulk because we didn't apply false lashes, nail extensions, or even a boob job.

We soon learnt to have a discussion with the mums when we took the booking to discuss the suitability for the child's age. If the girls were teens, we made sure we asked questions to ensure the party would be suitable for them. Equally, we would have to warn the mums of two and three-year-olds that they were far too young to sit and be pampered. What they really needed was to be bouncing around on an inflatable castle.

The mums were often more demanding than their children. As I mentioned before, the salon rule was no food to be eaten on the premises. Most parents took the children home for party food afterwards. Some, more affluent parents would take them off to the cinema, followed by pizzas.

But some mums would decide to ignore the no-food policy. They had decided that their little ones really couldn't wait for an hour or two without being fed, so brought along food regardless of the rules. We would politely ask them not to give the kids food but were often completely ignored. What could you do? Kick them all out and ruin the little one's party. Of course not. But whenever they treated us like that the party always ended earlier than usual. Funny that!

Some mums would tell us they were just popping across the road for a "quick coffee". They would turn up towards the end of the party, having obviously been to the lounge bar for a couple of wines with the other mums. They didn't give a hoot about our terms and conditions, which stated clearly that they were required to stay and supervise. Again, what could you do, send out a search party or throw the girls out? You could only tell them the rules and regulations and then it was up to them.

When we first started the parties, we would tell people the conditions on the telephone. Then later at the party we would have mums declaring that we hadn't told them about the rules they were breaking. After a few months, we were emailing written terms and conditions, so they couldn't say they didn't know.

Some parties were just a real special treat for the girls, and it was obvious that mum had struggled to pay for it. These were often the best parties and the most fun, with the girls really enjoying every minute. They always seemed more grateful and we always made sure there were some extra goodies in the girls' party bags to go home with.

The not so enjoyable parties were usually for the girls who turned up in pink limos, with their designer clothes, demanding to be treated like queens instead of princesses. Then they would spend the whole time competing against each other by boasting about future parties or holidays. They would brag about what they had or what they wanted, rather than enjoying the moment. In my opinion, these girls were the poorer ones; missing out on what it was like to just be little girls and have fun in the moment.

We were careful about making sure that the girls' parties were age appropriate. We were very aware of our responsibility to not make them feel less than perfect about the way they looked. We would always try to boost their confidence and tell them they were beautiful without any adornments. For us it was about having fun and making sure our little charges walked out the door still looking, and feeling, like pretty girls....and not mini adults.

Most of the time I loved the parties, it was a fun way to end the week in the salon.

When I had to take some time out from salon work (when my first husband and I split up) mobile parties became a nice little earner for me. Every weekend I would descend on various homes for a girlie birthday party. One added advantage of this mobile business was that my daughter gained a Saturday job. She was very artistic and great with hair and make-up, so this was perfect for her. It also stopped her performing any more Ouija board sessions while I was out of the house.

When I had my high street salon, we had age restrictions on treatments. Sometimes, this was for legal reasons. For instance, no one under the age of sixteen could have their ears pierced without an adult being present and parental consent.

However, we could also set our own standards, so decided not to pierce the ears of anyone under the age of eighteen without parental consent. As joint owners, we were both also parents, and as such would be upset if someone stuck a hole in our children's ears without our knowledge, even if they were sixteen.

We also felt we had moral obligations with some treatments. There was obviously the Brazillian and Hollywood waxing rules mentioned earlier. Parent's consent for teenagers was essential for this type of treatment.

What we could never understand were the parents asking for things that were completely unsuitable for their children, which would make the kids question their own natural beauty.

On more than one occasion a mother would stand in front of us demanding that their under sixteen-year-old be allowed to use the sunbed we originally had in the salon. Why would you damage your child's skin for the sake of a tan?

They would demand that as they had given their permission, we ought to let the child use the tanning machine. The law was on our side, but we also had a moral responsibility to the child. I'm sure these parents took their children elsewhere and got the harmful tan, but at least our conscience was clear.

Lots of ten and eleven-year-olds would come in and want nail extensions. We wouldn't carry out this treatment unless they were over sixteen, and even then, we would only do it for a special occasion and not all the time. These are chemicals that are applied to a growing child. The human nail absorbs products, especially a young child's thin nail plates. We would also explain to the parents that the girls would break the extensions and possibly damage their natural nails in the process.

Unfortunately, these mothers would not take our advice or refusal to do the treatment and go elsewhere. On more than one occasion they would return to us later from a disastrous visit to the chop shop begging for help.

I could never understand how parents who, even inadvertently, were basically saying to their girls, that they were less than perfect the way they were. I saw it on more than one occasion. They would make a little comment or a suggestion of having a treatment that would make their daughter, "look prettier."

The incident that really stands out to me was the mum who came in asking for her four-year-old to have a spray tan.

Now, we had spray tanned girls of nine and ten previously as they were going to be in a dance competition. This was practically the norm in the dance world. As it was only for the duration of the competition, we had no objections. Personally, I don't understand why the natural milky skin of a youngster wasn't perfection enough for the judges, but I also accepted that this was the way it was.

But why spray tan a four-year-old? The explanation was the girl was being christened and, in her mum's opinion, she was too pale for her white dress. She explained that a spray tan would give her some colour, and this would look better for the photographs. Her beautiful English rose wasn't the colour she wanted her to be. What was that mother saying to her little girl? Needless to say, we refused to do the treatment.

My girls grew up surrounded by the beauty industry. I always went out of my way to make them understand that beauty came from within. A cliché, I know, but I didn't want them to think that they had to have nail extensions, tans, and full-on make-up to look beautiful. In fact, as I said right at the beginning, I myself am exceptionally low maintenance; considering I could be done up to the nines with every beauty treatment out there if I chose. My girls are now adults and beautifully natural in their looks.

Back when I owned my own salon, I never really understood why people wanted their three-week-old baby's ears pierced either. I did do ear piercing but chose not to do it on babies. On the other hand, my colleague did pierce baby's ears, but only after they had been given all their inoculations.

She was incredibly good at it. She didn't want people going elsewhere to have lopsided holes put into their little one's ears. You needed a straight eye as you could only do one ear at a time, and the baby would never keep still long enough for most people to get the measurements right.

The mum would ask, "Will it hurt?" Of course, it hurts! You're putting a hole through their ear. "Will she cry?" Of course, she'll cry. You've just put a hole in her ear.

I used to hate seeing it done. You had to physically hold the baby's head in position as the gun punched a hole through the earlobe. Just holding the baby in this way made them cry. Often, the mother wasn't even there during the procedure, because she had nominated a friend or relative to do the deed for her.

All those years ago I was very against babies having their ears pierced. But having lived away from the UK since then I have come to realise that in some countries it's part of the culture. I now know that many Spanish families have their baby girls' ears pierced in the hospital, before they even go home. This is just a cultural tradition.

Although I am a bit more understanding now, I still can't get my head around why parents feel the need to put holes in these perfect little angels?

Treating children was not always about beautifying them. For instance, the little boy whose eyebrows and eyelashes we agreed to tint. He was about ten or eleven years old and had just started senior school. He was being teased and bullied because of his brows and lashes.

When he was about five, he came off his little push bike, hitting his head. No serious damage was done except, from that day onwards, half of his eyelashes and eyebrows on one side had no pigment and were completely white in colour.

Now, if the little boy had been fair haired it may have not have been quite so noticeable, but he had jet-black hair, and therefore jet-black lashes and brows. Everything had been fine until senior school and suddenly he had become very self-conscious because some horrible boys had started making fun of him.

So, we tinted his lashes, and he felt normal and blended in which, unfortunately, is important at that age. We felt good for helping him, although looking back years later I wish we had given him the treatment for free rather than charging his parents. That few pounds a month didn't really make or break the bank. I hope, as he got older, he was able to embrace his pure white hairs that made him look unique.

Fish & Feet

People would constantly say to me, "I don't know how you can touch feet. I couldn't?" But I prefer people's feet to their hands most of the time. When they come to see me for a pedicure, they usually arrive with their feet nice and clean and tucked up in their shoes ready for me to sort them out.

Hands, on the other hand, (excuse the pun) touch everything. All day, every day they get covered in a variety of bacteria. Not everyone washes their hands after using the toilet, picking up money or wiping a child's snotty nose. Therefore feet, to me, always seemed to be the cleaner option.

The word pedicure stems from Latin: Pes, meaning foot, and cura, which means care. There is evidence of people pampering their feet for more than 4,000 years. Carvings have been found in Egyptian pharaohs' tombs of people receiving manicures and pedicures.

In the 12th century, barbers would have bathing rooms which they used for shaving, as well as small surgical procedures. This would include pulling teeth and foot pampering, which often involved removing warts and corns. Thankfully, this combination of treatments is no longer available. I wouldn't fancy pulling teeth just before I put a nail polish on someone's tootsies, I can tell you.

Like the manicure, the pedicure can involve a lot of work to be done in a short amount of time. When feet have been neglected it can take a considerable amount of work to get them looking picture perfect again.

But amazing transformations can occur. Hard skin, tatty cuticles and uneven nail shapes turned into smooth, hydrated, beautiful feet with brightly coloured nails. It can be an extremely rewarding treatment for both therapist and client.

Hygiene is of the utmost importance when dealing with feet. They can easily pick up infections. Two common ones are verrucas, which are viral and can be caught from walking bare foot in swimming pools; and athlete's foot, which is a fungal infection.

Feet are tucked away in warm socks and work hard all day, supporting our body weight, getting a little sweaty. This is an ideal environment for fungal and bacterial infections. These types of infections can easily be passed from person to person, especially during pedicures.

It's essential that the therapist is scrupulously clean. They must make sure all the pedicure equipment is cleaned and sterilised between every client, to avoid cross contamination. If this isn't done the clients run the risk of picking up a bad infection, which can result in the need to remove a nail, or maybe worse. This is especially true if you have a health condition that causes slow healing.

I have known of salons that have extremely poor hygiene procedures in place. Check out the high street chop shops that have a conveyor belt of people putting their feet into unclean foot baths and using inadequately sterilised instruments on client after client.

Make sure your salon adheres to strict hygiene procedures. Don't feel bad about asking questions. Look after yourself. You want to have a great treatment; walking away with wonderful looking feet, not infections and health problems.

It's a therapist's job to make sure the client is healthy before proceeding with any treatment. We must always check for contraindications or contra-actions (reasons for not performing or for amending a set procedure).

Some clients are not happy about being turned away and will try to persuade you to carry on with the treatment. Some salon owners are also not happy when a therapist declines to carry out a treatment because it costs them money. As a professional therapist you must be assertive, which does get easier the more experienced and older you are.

You need to be diplomatic with clients. I never told any of them they definitely had an infection but would suggest they may have a problem; always recommending they get it checked out by a doctor or nurse. I would also reassure them that bacterial and fungal infections were common and not a result of being dirty. Most clients didn't even realise they had an infection and were grateful for the knowledge so they could get the problem sorted out.

The most severe and memorable fungal infection I saw was very extreme. I had a lady arrive who had been given a voucher. I welcomed her, and after discovering this was to be her first pedicure, explained the treatment. She proceeded to remove her shoes and socks and I popped my gloves on ready to inspect her feet.

Then I looked down and, at first glance, I thought she had black nail polish on her toes. Trendy, I thought. But then I smelt a strong odour that made me take a closer look.

Every toe had such a severe fungal infection that they had turned a dark green, almost black colour. The nails had started to crumble away, and it was obvious this was a fungal infection that was literally eating her toes away. I was so shocked… I'm sure I just stared with my mouth open.

I told the lady she had a severe infection and she needed to see the doctor urgently. I was astonished that she had not realised. As I talked to her, I soon realised the lady had some learning difficulties, and she was shocked to hear that she had a problem. We also found out that this voucher had been bought by a friend she went swimming with. We thought maybe this was the friend's diplomatic way of telling her she had a problem. She assured us she would go to the doctors, and I suggested we did a manicure instead, as I knew her feet were going to be a problem that would not be fixed quickly.

People often apologised when showing me their feet, and so many people hated something about them. Too big, too long, too fat, or funny shaped toes. There were very few people who loved their feet.

I've seen many different shapes and sizes of feet, all just waiting to be pampered. Some had missing toes, while others were so perfect, they were signed up with modelling agencies.

I remember working on one lady's feet and some of her toes were webbed. Before I painted her nails, I needed to separate them. Unlike most therapists, I favoured separating the toes with folded tissue rather than the pre-made toe separators.

There were two main reasons for my choice. Tissues are disposable so there are no issues with cross contamination, and everyone's toes are different sizes. The 'one size fits all' toe separators don't always fit everyone comfortably, and this would have been even more apparent in this lady's case.

I gently placed the folded tissue between my client's toes, avoiding the webbed toes, as you could obviously not part these. The lady immediately said, "You're the only therapist that hasn't tried to stick toe separators in there." She laughed as she told me how highly amusing she found it when therapists desperately tried to separate her webbed toes. Common sense is essential in any job.

Talking about webbed feet; never in a million years did I think fish would become part of my beauty business. I love yummy salmon on my plate, but live fish, in a tank, in my salon? Shut that door!

We first read about it in a London magazine; *the fish pedicure* was all the rage. You would place your feet in a tank of tropical water and the fish would nibble off the dead skin. And so, began my journey into fish pedicures.

Garra Rufa Fish, also known as Doctor Fish, were first brought to the western world for the treatment of psoriasis – a skin condition that has a build-up of dead skin cells. The fish would gently eat away at the dead skin, helping to improve the uncomfortable condition.

The fish were used as a gentle way to remove the skin, rather than harsh scrubbing tools or products that could cause severe reaction in these clients. As these things tend to go, the mainstream beauty industry decided it was also a great way to have ordinary hard skin removed from the feet.

We started to investigate the effects of the treatment after we read about it in the magazine and were impressed with the results. So, we decided to introduce fish to the salon.

At this time, it was a very new treatment and we couldn't find any companies that supplied either the tank, or the fish. So, we went to the experts.

We went to a local garden centre and found a chap who had kept, bred, and sold tropical and marine fish forever.

I think he thought we were completely mad when we asked him if he could help us set up a tropical fish tank so people could put their feet into it - and charge them for the privilege. He was intrigued by these two nutty beauty therapists and agreed to help us. He ended up being our go-to fish man and helped us look after our fish for a couple of years.

The first tank was literally just that, a tank. We had a comfy chair that people sat on and they had to lift their feet up and into the tank. But after just a couple of months, and thanks to our wonderful fish man, we had a purpose-built chair and tank set-up specifically for our fish pedicures. We were the first salon in the West Country to have the fish pedicure and made the local paper – which was all exceptionally good for business.

For our fish man, and for us, the fish's well-being was always our chief concern. So, he taught us how to look after them, and would come regularly to check the PH of the water, and that the fish were thriving. He was also our fish doctor when they didn't feel very well, which fortunately, was not very often.

We were very fussy about whose feet went into the water. No one with open cuts, abrasions, skin disorders or nail polish went in with our fish.

We would wash the client's feet with special soapy water and rinse them before they were placed into the tank. During this initial soak we would also inspect the skin to make sure it was not going to make our fish poorly. The fish would nibble at the feet for ten to twenty minutes. When they had their fill, we finished the treatment with a relaxing foot and leg massage.

We were extremely strict and made sure that when our clients booked, they knew what we expected from them. As always, there were the clients who tried to ignore our warnings about nail polish, cuts, and abrasions. Some of them would get really upset when we told them they couldn't have their treatment. But our attitude was that we were responsible for these fish, and we were not going to kill them for the sake of a beauty treatment.

Again, what was initially a chat on the phone later became an email containing our terms and conditions.

As a lot of people will remember, this treatment became very mainstream, and suddenly there were whole shops just dedicated to the fish pedicure. Even in shopping malls, you could take your shoes and socks off and just dip your feet into a warm fish tank.

These kinds of places were all about the money. They didn't bother washing anyone's feet or inspecting them for cuts or contagious conditions such as athlete's foot.

The fish in these shops were treated very cruelly. They were just a commodity. They did the job and then were discarded as if they were nothing. These places had new fish delivered when required, often daily. Due to the conditions they were kept in they never lived long. They would also have hundreds of tiny fish in one tank.

On the other hand, we had some of our fish for the whole two years we offered the treatment. In our large tank we would only have around twenty-five fish. In this way, they mostly grew and thrived, and we got a real kick out of watching them grow. We got really upset if we lost a fish.

Clients would question how many fish we had in our tank, and we would explain that our fish had the right amount of space to thrive, and as they were much bigger, they could eat more. The crowded tanks were cruel as the fish would die daily without ever being given a chance to thrive and grow.

There was also a high risk of cross contamination in these places, as anyone could put their feet in with a contagious disease and pass it on to the next person. No one ever checked for contra-indications, and nor did they care if the fish were nibbling nail polish. All these things meant those poor fish never lasted long. It got to the point that you had problems getting hold of them. They were being over fished in a most barbaric way.

Our fish became our pets; we would greet them in the morning and say goodnight to them in the evening. We would call the fish man if they seemed off colour and would cancel treatments if they were not up to a day of nibbling. We got used to knowing how many treatments they could do in a day and ensured they had proper rest breaks.

They could still let us down though. If they decided they didn't like someone's feet, there was nothing we could do to encourage them to get to work and nibble. "Why aren't they nibbling my feet?" clients would ask.

I could never say why. They just didn't like some people's feet; and it wasn't that they weren't hungry, as they would eat the next pair of feet without a problem. We could have fish pedicures booked all day, and the fish just wouldn't play ball. All we could do was cancel clients and refund their money.

Clients would also come in and say they needed a specific bit of hard skin removed. We would have to explain that the fish nibbled where they wanted, and we couldn't make them attack a certain area. They weren't trainable!

So many different types of people wanted to try the fish pedicure. Late evenings and Saturdays the fish were rushed off their fins!

All walks of life wanted one. Ticklish people would win bets on whether they could keep their feet in the water for the duration of the treatment. They would sit cringing and laughing for the full fifteen minutes, just to win the money.

People would spend ten minutes just plucking up the courage to put their feet in the water. There were those who thought they would be fine, only to discover that they couldn't stand the treatment for more than five seconds once it started.

Did I enjoy having the treatment myself?

No. It gave me the shivers having these little fish nibbling between my toes and around my heels. I found it extremely irritating, and though I tried it out a couple of times, I hated it.

Not long after having them, I received a phone call from a lady asking if I would like to bring my fish to WOMAD – The World of Music and Dance Festival. This festival was hosted about ten miles from Bath, and I thought this lady was mad for asking me. I had been to lots of music festivals, and couldn't work out how my fish would fit in.

She explained that they ran a tented spa area, and the fish would be a great add-on to the normal massage and facials that were on offer.

I love a good music festival and thought it would be a great PR opportunity for the salon. So, after having a word with my fish man, confirming the fish's welfare and transport, I called the lady back and told her to expect a tank of fish to grace her Arabian Night style spa.

One Wednesday evening in June, I headed over to Charlton Park with my husband and set up our tent, ready to receive my fish the next morning.

The fish man picked up the fish and the equipment in Bath on the Thursday morning, and transported them to me at the festival. We proceeded to set everything up in the tented spa. This was a huge tent, with sectioned-off massage areas, lounging areas, and bars, as well as lovely hot showers and nice loos. It even had some open-air Jacuzzis. It was all done out in a

Moroccan style, and we all wore sarongs embellished with the WOMAD logo.

I spent the first day letting my fish settle in and keeping an eye on them, checking the water temperature and PH levels. Then, I settled into a continual run of dirty festival feet coming in the door wanting to be revived. I had to wash their feet, and in some cases scrub them, before I would let them anywhere near my fish.

Every morning I had to walk to an outside tap and fill buckets of water ready to clean people's feet. I literally had to boil a full kettle of water for each new client. The fish and I would work for four hours, and then we would have a break for a couple of hours. I would grab a bite to eat, and my fish would regain their appetites ready for the afternoon session.

It was pretty hard work, and although I got to listen to some good music, I couldn't really let my hair down as I was constantly checking on the fish, making especially sure that the electricity was running for them. Because of this, I was the only one allowed past the security guards at night; and they would shout out, "Here comes the fish lady!"

We even had the Earl of Suffolk, who owned the estate, come and grace us with his feet. My fish nibbled the common person as well as near royalty.

The fish pedicure died a death overnight after a damming report on the front page of *The Sun* newspaper. The report had a lot of truth in it about cross contamination, how the fish were being completely exploited and how cruel it all was. However, it was all one sided, and it didn't consider the salons like us that were doing it right and had only given these fish the chance to do what they do naturally.

Did we miss the fish when they went? No, not really. They were hard work to keep, and as with any pet or animal, were a big responsibility.

Did we enjoy the whole process? Absolutely, it was a fun treatment to introduce and we were proud that we were one of the first salons to offer the treatment. We looked after our fish extremely well and on the day they left the salon, many of them were the same fish that we started with on day one…. all grown-up.

Happy work, happy days

I know some people consider my work shallow, but my job has always, and continues to, bring me great joy – so it's not shallow to me.

I've spent my working days looking after people and making them feel special. I've performed treatments to relax them, to make them feel better about themselves and have even sorted out issues that were profoundly affecting their happiness and confidence.

I've had the honour of meeting lots of different people, sharing their life experiences and being part of their journey. I've also been lucky enough to use lots of wonderful products and beautiful smelling oils every day. There have always been new and exciting treatments, products, and ideas to keep things fresh and interesting for me too.

Having to put a happy face on every day has, inadvertently, kept me feeling upbeat and positive throughout my thirty-year career. My job has often made me appreciate all that I have in my own life;

making me realise I am truly rich – even if that hasn't always meant financially.

My advice to my children many years ago was to choose a profession or job that would bring them joy. We spend a huge amount of our life at work, and it's a lot easier doing it every day if we enjoy it. I have certainly done that!

All these things, I think, are reasons why I've enjoyed being a beauty therapist so much; and probably explain why so many people think this is one of the happiest professions to work in.

Ultimately, the number one reason I love my job is, of course, because of the clients. They have all made my working life fun, interesting, rewarding, and hugely memorable.

I want all my clients to know that every one of you has brought me such joy over the years. Knowing you has made me a better person. In my saddest days, going to work and being with all of you - *my ladies* - often made the difficult times so much more bearable. My working life has been extremely rewarding and so much fun.

Thank you from the bottom of my heart.

Wendy x

What Now?

Now we are back living in the UK, I'm concentrating on my first love, The Skin. I am continually updating my qualifications and skills and moving further into the aesthetic industry.

I have a Facebook group where you can find lots of yummy information on the skin and how to look after yours.

If you'd like to come and hang out with me, I'd love to see you on the inside!

https://www.facebook.com/groups/facial expert

Acknowledgements

This is the part where you have a never-ending list of people you thank, and nobody reads it apart from people looking for their names. Of course, I've got people to thank, but I am going to keep it simple. There are many friends and family who have encouraged and supported me on my writing journey. You know who you are, and I thank you.

Thank you, Abigail Moss, for your first edit which made me look at a few topics in a different light.

Also, to my wonderful friend Vicky, (Victoria Crumpton) who has been my main go-to for encouragement and honesty throughout the process. Also, for her editing and recommendations to make my little book better

I huge thank you to my husband, John. For putting up with my mini tantrums when the technology didn't work (when I normally got it wrong). For your patience, every time I messed up and panicked, for every word I have asked you to spell and your help throughout with editing. You are the one on the front line, the one who must put everything right for me. And you do, mostly with a smile.

My three children, Harriet, Georgina, and Jacob. Without you in my life, I would have just had a career.... instead of the wonderful adventure it turned out to be.

And, as always, thank you to every client who, over the years, told me that I should write a book.

I DID!

Printed in Great Britain
by Amazon